MORE THAN A GAME: 60 Stories of Character in Competition

A 12-Week Challenge for Today's Athlete

BY

REBEKAH TRITTIPOE

Praise for *More Than a Game*

In the pursuit of excellence in competition and life, talent is never enough. *More Than a Game* identifies with wonderful, real life, short story scenarios, the major factors that impact our pursuit to excellence. I loved that in the face of adversity, each story illustrates biblical truths that give clear direction to the next path. There is a brilliant progression of character development blended into the real world experiences and application of God's Word. Rebekah Trittipoe, while entertaining, provides an excellent blue print to build the character of a champion who is in pursuit of excellence. This is an exceptional book written by an exceptional athlete, coach, guide, wife, mom, and person.

~ CoachCarey Green

Former Head Coach, Women's Basketball, Liberty University

15 NCAA Tournament Appearances,

15 NCAA D1 Conference Championships

As a lifelong competitor and now a coach, I believe sport is the greatest platform of influence in modern culture—for better or for worse! In *More Than a Game* you will find a game plan to keep the "main thing the main thing." It's about more than great performance; it's about encouraging others to be great people—fulfilling their God-given purpose for life!

~ Jimmy Page

Chief Leadership Officer, SportsLife Leadership

Former VP of Field Ministry, Fellowship of Christian Athletes (FCA)

In today's competitive world of athletics, the coach that is truly in it for the right reason, is the one who is looking to use the life lessons learned through the sport to develop his athletes: physically, intellectually, socially and spiritually. This fast-moving, well-organized book takes the team through a proactive look at the highs and the lows that they will experience through their involvement in sports and how God wants them to use the experiences to turn their focus to Him.

~ Coach Frank Rocco

Head Coach, Liberty Christian Academy

6 State Championships, 250 Wins

Rebekah Trittipoe's *More Than a Game* is an amazing resource for a coach, team member, or individual athlete who wants to be faithful with the talents they've been given. A highly recommended read!

~ Josh Cox

Former 50K American Record Holder, Sports Agent

More Than a Game is a wonderful resource for teams or individual athletes looking for a concise tool to help focus the spiritual and mental components of their season. The format is easy to use and strikes a nice balance in its brief yet engaging daily content.

~ Chris Anderson

Former Director, Fellowship of Christian Athletes Endurance Ministry

Regional Director of Talent Acquisition, FCA

One of the greatest temptations for the Christian athlete is to seek her own purposes or run for personal glory, and *More Than a Game* is the perfect antidote to this. Rebekah Trittipoe—one of the East Coast's most highly regarded "trail moms" and respected competitors—provides a unique resource for athletes, teams, and coaches that instructs us to thoughtfully engage our athletic commitments within the context of our Christian faith. The text is lively and articulate, scripturally supported, fun, and full of stories and activities that lead us to think through what it means to glorify God in running. I highly recommend this devotional for teams who want to know what the Bible says about athletic disciplines and to serve God more fully through their sport.

~ Sabrina (Moran) Little

Former 24-hour run American Record Holder

When you start any journey, it is important to have the end in mind. In this book, Coach Trittipoe not only leads the reader to consider the end of the season or the end of the athletic career, but the end product of a life that is lived well for the Lord. Rebekah reminds us of the great biblical life lessons that can be learned though athletics, especially when carefully guided by a committed Christian coach. Regardless of the W's and L's, your season will be positive as you follow *More Than a Game.*

~ Coach Brant Tolsma

Former Liberty University Head Track and Field/CC Coach,

2010 World Age-group Double Decathlon Record Holder

Seasoned coach or beginning your career, an avid athlete or novice team member, this book can arm you with valuable life skills beyond the next race. As a respected, exceptional, and experienced ultrarunner and coach, Rebekah Trittipoe offers a life changing perspective on athletics and all that sport can teach us about ourselves; inspiring us as individuals, mentors, coaches, and teammates to help us discover our potential. I highly recommend *More Than a Game* as I believe it can be the most important resource in your coaching inventory.

~ Jennifer Anderson

Coach and Ultrarunner,

Overall record holder, Camino de Santiago, Spain

There is no shortcut to success. It takes a solid game plan. A game plan that comes from both research and real world experience. That is what Coach Trittipoe provides through *More Than a Game* ... it is a blueprint to reaching one's true POTENTIAL inside!

~ Scotty Curlee

Director/Producer, *The Potential Inside* movie,

Former professional cyclist

As an athlete, I know that the most important lessons that I learned on the court, and as part of a team, are lessons that can be translated into character, relationships, and faith. But that does not mean those lessons are easy to talk about or convey—especially without sounding corny or condescending.

Rebekah seemingly does the impossible by making these universal values of Christian faith and athletics come across as sounding cool and conversational. Her short daily anecdotes alternate between 3,000-year-old biblical stories and modern day sports feats, allowing the lessons of faith to feel both timeless and relevant.

~ Jennifer Pharr Davis

Former Speed Record Holder, Appalachian Trail,

Author/Speaker

Rebekah Trittipoe's book, *More Than a Game*, is a powerfully moving book that will make you forget you are reading a book for coaches. Be prepared to have a heart examination. The group dynamics, stories, and Scripture readings are like pearls of wisdom woven into daily practices. These super tools can build or renew any team's foundation. This book is written with a passion for today's youth. If you want to experience greater love in coaching, read *More Than a Game.* If you want to build godly character in your team, read *More Than a Game.* If you want a dose of perseverance, read *More Than a Game.* I did.

~ Susan Morgan

Former Collegiate All-American and Distance Coach

The beginning of the season for every sports team brings with it excitement and high expectations for success! Many teams begin the season strong but often fail to maintain that momentum as the season progresses. Rebekah Trittipoe has written an amazing book on how to keep you and your team focused when it hurts and when you are facing the grind and challenges of a long season. Rebekah isn't writing from an opinion or something she researched; rather as a world-class athlete she's writing from the blood, sweat and tears of her own experience!

~ Aaron Davis

Motivational speaker, Author,

Member of the 1994 National Championship Nebraska football team

MORE THAN A GAME: 60 STORIES OF CHARACTER IN COMPETITION -
A 12 Week Challenge for Today's Athlete
By Rebekah Trittipoe
Published by Twisted Trails Publishing
2527 Triggs Rd, Bedford, VA 24523

ISBN 978-1-7370899-4-0

Cover design by HannahLinderDesigns
https://hannahlinderdesigns.com/

Formerly published as "Best Season Yet: 12 Weeks to Train" by Rebekah Trittipoe
Lighthouse Publishing of the Carolinas, 2013

For more information on this book and the author visit:
https://rebekahtrittipoe.com
http://rebekahtrittipoe.blogspot.com/
Printed in the United States of America

TWISTED TRAILS
PUBLISHING

Table of Contents

Dedication

Alana Desris was my first coach—gymnastics. Emily David taught me the game of field hockey. Merv Bryan set me up to fly around a track. June Kearney molded me as a college volleyball player while Pamela Diehl Johnson and Dee Morris tuned up my tennis game. But my athletic training started way before any of these coaches wrote my name on their rosters.

You could safely say my family was athletic. My Dad was a college baseball player and spent a lifetime on the tennis court. My mom was game for recreational tennis and hit the slopes in the winter along with the rest of the family. My brothers—David, Dan, and John—were all standout athletes in high school and college. After college, David turned pro in tennis, Dan gained notoriety on the racquetball court, and John became an accomplished ultramarathoner. Being a non-athlete wasn't even a choice for me.

My family is a blessing. I learned many a life lesson playing Wiffle ball on a Sunday afternoon with Dad, my brothers, and all the neighborhood kids we could find. When the weather turned cool, I remember suiting up in a Philadelphia Eagles football uniform, shoulder pads and helmet included, to play a game of backyard touch. And when falling off the beam in a gymnastics meet discouraged me, Dad always said, "DeLanceys never quit." He was right. I didn't.

So I dedicate this book to my family of athletes. A family that played together and prayed together. I am who I am by the grace of God. But by the grace of God I learned a little something about life through running, jumping, hitting balls, and flipping with my family.

Thanks, Mom and Dad (who watch from above), David, Dan, and John. Thanks for letting this girl play.

Foreword

I spent three days on the trail with Rebekah Trittipoe during the summer of 2011. She was part of the crew that successfully helped me set the overall Appalachian Trail Record—at 46 days, 11 hours, and 20 minutes, an average of 46.9 miles per day. I never could have accomplished this goal without a huge support network, and Rebekah proved to be one of the most helpful and joyful members of our team. She was a constant motivator and encourager. And her strong faith helped refresh my spirit on a daily basis.

Rebekah's skill set is perfectly suited to be a coach. I believe this is due to her natural God-given talents and furthermore enhanced by years of instructing student athletes to do their best on and off the field. When I had the opportunity to read her book, *More Than a Game: 60 Stories of Character in Competition*, I was impressed by how well her experience and personality came through in this very well-written guide. I immediately thought of multiple coaches, teachers, and even parents who would love to incorporate the lessons of this book into a fun and interactive three-month study.

As an athlete, I know that the most important lessons I learned on the court, and as part of a team, are lessons that can be translated into character, relationships, and faith. But that does not mean those lessons are easy to talk about or convey—especially without sounding corny or condescending. Rebekah seemingly does the impossible by making the universal values of Christian faith and athletics sound cool and conversational. Her short daily anecdotes alternate between 3,000-year-old biblical stories and modern day sports feats, allowing the lessons of faith to feel both timeless and relevant.

Rebekah has succeeded in making this book both practical and engaging. The daily lessons are concise and can be incorporated in less than five to ten minutes of practice time. In fact, the daily passage could be read to a team during pre-practice stretches or a post-workout cool-down. No matter when and how the book is shared, athletes will always be participants in the devotional because of her weekly team-building activities and moments for reflection.

Regardless of your final record, I truly believe that if coaches implement *More Than a Game* into their daily practice routine for twelve weeks, they will forever impact the character and faith of their athletes—and will undoubtedly experience a winning season.

Jennifer Pharr Davis
World record holder, Appalachian Trail, author and speaker

Preface

People often ask me why I run. It's a simple question with a complex answer. Just ask one of my athletes. The other day she wore a t-shirt bearing this phrase: "If you have to ask me why I run, don't bother." Snide and haughty perhaps, but it implies there is something deeply spiritual about the act of putting one foot in front of another. It also suggests that some people just don't "get it."

So, why do I run? For that matter, why did I play sports all through my high school and college years? Why persist in leagues and competitions as an adult? I used to glibly answer, "Because I can." But not now.

While it's true that I can run, I've realized that a better answer would be, "Because God made me this way." There's a big difference. No. A huge difference.

If you're reading this book, you're probably either a coach or an athlete. Maybe even both. You likely have a higher than normal level of interest and athletic ability. You may have also grappled with the very same question. What's *your* answer?

I've always approached athletics—as a participant and coach—as a way to mature spiritually. Sports teach so many lessons about steadfastness, staying the course, perseverance, and wholeheartedness. We equate the toils of training as opportunities to "press on" and "run the race with patience" (Philippians 3:12-14; Hebrews 12:2).

There's nothing wrong with using athletic analogies. The writers of Scripture used this parallelism to make concepts more understandable. However, when thinking about God's sovereignty, I've come to realize that His purpose was to make me athletic, to make me a runner. It didn't happen by accident. I relate to Eric Liddle, the Scottish Olympian who is quoted in *Chariots of Fire*: "I believe God made me for a purpose, but He also made me fast. When I run, I feel His pleasure."

Why is that? Is it so I can set records? So I can be in great shape? While those things might happen, I suggest those are not reason enough. The reason God made me a runner was to equip me to ultimately reflect His character.

I have to look at my athletic endeavors as a means to an end, not a means unto itself. If I can run to present Christ to people, then I will run. If I can set trail records so it gives me a platform to write a book about God's faithfulness, then I will go to the woods.

I suggest we consider our athletic endeavors, whether they are individual or team-based, as a gift—a means to God's end. This book will lead us through an entire season of training. It will help us understand commitment, challenge, pain and suffering, fear and dreams, excellence, team dynamics, goals, and physical, emotional, and spiritual gains in the context of advancing the kingdom of God.

Ready. Set. Go.

There are different kinds of gifts, but the same Spirit. There are different kinds of service, but the same Lord. There are different kinds of working, but the same God works all of them in all men. All these are the work of one and the same Spirit, and he gives them to each one, just as he determines (1 Corinthians 12:4-6, 11).

Week 1: Can-do Commitments, Day 1

Oh, boy. Here goes nothing.

So, here you are. You decided to come out for the team. For some of you, it's a novel event. You really aren't sure what to expect. For others, you've been there, done that. Regardless of whether you're a newbie or veteran, this season has the potential to be so much better than any other. Accept the challenges—all of them—and see if you come out the other side a more complete athlete. Maybe even a more complete person.

A certain amount of courage is needed to begin any undertaking. And the more committed you are, the more courage you need. Questions swirl in your head:

- *Do I have what it takes?*
- *Will I be in the starting lineup?*
- *Can I handle the practice schedule?*
- *Am I fit enough?*
- *What if I get injured?*
- *Can I handle academics and athletics at the same time?*
- *What if the coach is a moron and I hate him/her?*

Want to hear a story? Back in the early to mid '70s, girls didn't have many options for organized sport. No community T-ball or soccer. No basketball. In fact, not until a certain girl reached the ninth grade was she allowed to try out for any team. So, try out she did. The high school offered only one fall sport for girls: field hockey. On that hot and humid August afternoon, Rebekah was assigned a stick. Though the athlete wannabe had no idea what to do with it, she had just begun a long-term athletic adventure.

The school and fields, situated on steep terraces, were put to good use. Up and down the inclines the team raced, sticks in hand. Their legs ached and their lungs screamed for the misery to end. The coach didn't always tell them how much or how long they would run. The girls just kept running until she said "stop," and then they gladly sucked down salty water. No Gatorade back then. Then they did it again. Most of them accepted the challenge of those sweltering three-a-day summer practices and made it to season's end—a goal worth reaching in so many ways.

You might as well know up front that you won't always "feel" like practicing. The schedule may interfere with your social calendar. You might not cherish the aching muscles. But accepting the challenge will also produce feelings of accomplishment and opportunities to learn, grow, and excel. But understand this. Ultimately, it's your full commitment to God that will equip you to commit to your best season yet.

Team Truth: *And may your hearts be fully committed to the LORD our God, to live by his decrees and obey his commands, as at this time.* (1 Kings 8:61)

Team Time: List three things to which each individual must commit if the team as a whole is to be successful.

1. ____
2. ____
3. ____

Week 1: Can-do Commitments, Day 2

Just say yes

"Coach." He shifted nervously and looked down at the floor. "I won't be able to be at practice on Wednesdays, and I'll also be gone every other Friday for drum lessons. Just wanted you to know." He spoke matter-of-factly and then, not waiting for a response, turned and slinked away, leaving the coach in stunned silence.

Why was he so nervous in breaking the news? And why was it more of a statement than a conversation? Maybe that athlete knew something was wrong. Either you're fully committed to the task at hand or you're not.

Miss Desris towered over the gymnasts with her "big-boned" 6 foot 2 inch frame. Though they loved and respected her, the nimble athletes were petrified to inform "Miss D," their gymnastics coach, of injury or illness. She didn't take kindly to excuses and she never, ever accepted an absence graciously. Just one uncomfortable stare-down from her scowling face was enough to put an end to any thought of breaking a commitment to the team.

Have we lost the ideal of being fully committed? Societal expectations pressure us to fill every minute of our lives with one thing or another. But it's impossible to serve more than one master at the same time. Jesus said so: "No one can serve two masters. Either you will hate the one and love the other, or you will be devoted to the one and despise the other" (Matthew 6:24a).

Don't misunderstand. Our top commitment should be to please God. Nothing should stand in the way. But that same principle teaches us something about making commitments. Promising a full commitment can be difficult. It should never be made lightly. A broken commitment is paramount to a lie—a lie to yourself, your coach, and your teammates. Those lies, like a rotten wood foundation, will jeopardize the stability of your team's foundation of trust and community. In fact, those lies and that lack of commitment can destroy your team.

Still, don't let the fear of failure or the unknown derail your desire to make that commitment. Apprehension is a natural emotion. But when you say "yes," mean it. There's no middle ground. No such thing as partial commitment.

Team Truth: *Above all, my brothers and sisters, do not swear—not by heaven or by earth or by anything else. All you need to say is a simple "Yes" or "No." Otherwise you will be condemned.* (James 5:12)

Team Time: What specific things might compete for your allegiance this season? Are you still willing to fully commit to this team?

____

____

____

____

____

____

____

____

____

____

Week 1: Can-do Commitments, Day 3

Commitment's not for weenies

Jennifer Anderson made a life-altering decision in 2010. The thirty-six-year-old wife, mother to three kids, full-time Spanish teacher and department head, decided to undertake an extreme adventure. A talented ultrarunner with many outstanding race performances, Jenny challenged Spain's Camino de Santiago Trail to a duel in February of 2011.

The Camino de Santiago Trail is a thousand-year-old, 507.8 mile long footpath that starts in the French village of Saint-Jean-Pied-de-Por and climbs over the Pyrenees Mountains into Spain, following the traditional way of Saint James and ending at the place of his burial. Thousands traverse "The Way" (as it is called) every year but do so leisurely and in good weather. This determined woman, however, had a mere ten days to travel it—in severe conditions that included high winds, snow, sleet, and near constant rain. Nine days, five hours, and twenty-nine minutes after she started her passage on foot, she arrived at the cathedral in Santiago de Compostela. An amazing feat. But probably not as amazing as what it took to realize that commitment.

Jenny knew that achieving this mark was difficult. She wasn't a paid athlete with her days free to train and prepare. She was a professional woman with school-aged children and many responsibilities. In order to put in the requisite training, she often rose at 3:00 a.m. to run twenty or thirty miles, laden down with a backpack, before waking the children to start their days. It didn't matter if it was raining, blustery, or frigid. She knew that accomplishing the task would require sacrifice and steadfastness. She kept her eye on the goal in order to get herself out the door, to coax her body into submission. That's commitment.

Not many athletes are called to such extreme endeavors and levels of commitment, but no individual can be a true athlete without commitment. Though the goal will define what our commitment should be, commitment keeps us focused. Commitment enables us to embrace the training and sacrifice. Without commitment, we're merely casual participants.

It was God's pleasure to make us athletes and offer us a platform to direct attention back to Him. Sure, the Christian athlete should be committed to his sport and to his team. But he must first and foremost be committed to his Father God.

Define the task. Commit to it. Allow God to strengthen you.

Team Truth: *For the eyes of the LORD range throughout the earth to strengthen those whose hearts are fully committed to him.* (2 Chronicles 16:9a)

Team Time: List at least one physical and one spiritual commitment you're willing to make this season. Write it down, share it with a teammate, and ask that person to hold you accountable.

Spiritual commitment: ______________________________

____

____

____

____

____

____

Physical commitment: ______________________________

____

____

____

____

____

____

Week 1: Can-do Commitments, Day 4

Wall Building 101

In the fifth century BC, Artaxerxes, king of Persia, was in the twentieth year of his reign. A Hebrew slave named Nehemiah served as cupbearer to the king, thus having the inside scoop on all things kingdom-related. Not escaping his notice was the newsflash that his beloved Jerusalem was in total disrepair. The walls had been demolished and gates burned. The city had crumbled—an unacceptable state for the centerpiece of Jewish culture. So a seed was planted in Nehemiah's mind: he'd go to Jerusalem to rebuild and restore.

But he needed help. He sought the king's approval and gained permission to travel through the territory and to gather supplies. He knew the gigantic task would be daunting. However, he didn't realize how much of a commitment he'd have to make.

When Nehemiah arrived at the war-torn city, his heart broke and his tears flowed. The damage was far worse than he had imagined. For three days he surveyed the situation and on the third night, stole away on a horse to be alone. Nehemiah wrote, "I had not told anyone what my God had put in my heart to do for Jerusalem" (Nehemiah 2:12). In the darkness, he was accompanied only by his commitment to fulfill God's plan.

Can you imagine the organization and skill it took to rebuild Jerusalem? No power tools. No bulldozers. No steel beams or pre-made bricks. Plus, ruthless opposition came from those who wanted the Jews to fail. But Nehemiah told them, "The God of heaven will give us success" (Nehemiah 2:20).

Continued threats and assaults during the rebuilding process caused headaches for Nehemiah's team. He wrote, "They were all trying to frighten us, thinking, 'Their hands will get too weak for the work, and it will not be completed'" (Nehemiah 6:9a).

Nehemiah's response? "Now strengthen my hand," he prayed (Nehemiah 6:9b). Then he persevered. The city was rebuilt, the people returned, and the God of Israel was honored.

Can you see some important lessons in this story? There are many, but among them are these two: First, commitments are seldom easy to keep. We must think through many details and face difficulties head on. Second, we may have to take a lonely ride through the scary darkness, alone with our thoughts and goals, to confirm our mission. In a society that idolizes constant social networking and limitless noise, we must understand that being alone is necessary so that we can focus our attention on what needs to be accomplished.

Let's not be afraid to go to a quiet place to search our hearts, our lives, our motives, our commitments.

Team Truth: *He says, "Be still, and know that I am God."* (Psalm 46:10a)

Team Time: Take a few minutes to look inward. Turn off the noise. Go to a quiet place alone. What is your Jerusalem? What is God asking you to commit to this season?

____

____

____

____

____

____

____

____

Week 1: Can-do Commitments, Day 5

Commitment by the chunk

We've spent a lot of time this week thinking about commitments and the seriousness of making them. In the process, we've read about some massive commitments folks have made. Those kinds of commitments can be as frightening as the prospect of jumping out of an airplane—without a parachute.

"But how in the world can I make that kind of commitment when I'm playing JV soccer?" you might ask. Or, "I'm not important, not a standout. I have little to contribute. All this talk about commitment is meaningless for me."

Is it really meaningless? Probably not. We tend to think of a commitment as something that is huge and momentous, but it doesn't have to be.

Let's say you're a runner going out for the cross country team. In the first time trial of the season, you turn in a time of 25:46 for the 5 km course. Trouble is, to make it into the top seven and run varsity, you will need to pull off at least a 22:25. So, you mentally commit to that goal. You show up for every practice, go through the required paces, stop eating so much ice cream, and run 25:38 at the next outing. Nowhere near your goal. You become so discouraged you quit. You think, *What's the sense of trying? I'll never cut away that much time.*

But as "they" say (whoever "they" are), Rome wasn't built in a day—and neither will you immediately see the fruit of your commitments. A commitment is a promise to yourself, a guiding light to some chosen finish line. However, a commitment has many layers and you must accomplish each one before moving on to the next. Your small improvements along the way will indicate that you're still on Commitment Road. Don't be discouraged. As long as you make forward progress and see more mileage posts along the way, you'll eventually reach the proper exit.

It might be better to see our commitments in terms of daily "chunks" rather than as one overwhelming and unobtainable feat. We must learn to run long and play strong—one step at a time.

Team Truth: *The simple believe anything, but the prudent give thought to their steps.* (Proverbs 14:15)

Team Time: Take a few minutes to break down your overall commitments to this season into smaller, more manageable goals. Define the intermediate steps necessary to accomplish your long-term goals. These can be personal and/or team commitments.

Week 2: Surrendering to Submission, Day 1

Seriously, do I have to?

The team gathered around, sitting cross-legged in front of their coach. Chatter, laughter, and jokes rippled through the crowd as they waited for practice to begin. It had been a tough day. But now, academics aside, the team members welcomed the physical release. All but one.

David wasn't happy to be there. Everyone knew that. Because he was an outstanding athlete, the school had convinced him to enroll and had supplied a full scholarship in return for his contribution to the athletic program. Just one little problem: David refused to be part of the team. His private coach provided training instructions, which David highly regarded at the expense of anything and everything the school's coach asked him to do. Consequently, he chose to train on his own, cherry-picked the meets to run, and even traveled separately from the rest of the team. The school's coach, in David's eyes, was a total moron. That explained the glare in his eyes—he resented that he'd been forced to attend this team meeting. He couldn't stand to be around these "amateurs," as he called them. David sat apart from the group, scowling. School administration looked the other way. The coach was frustrated, his authority undermined.

Though this may be a rare (but true) scenario, what is less rare is the subtle rebellion that many athletes display. Somehow, we think we know better than the coach. We assume that we really don't have to do everything he says. So we slow down when he's not looking, do twelve burpees instead of fifteen, or take a short cut once we're out of sight. *What he doesn't know won't hurt him,* we rationalize.

But there's something bigger we need to understand. By becoming part of a team, we've chosen a position of submission. We've willingly placed ourselves under the authority of the coach. Serious stuff. For our submission to the authority of Jesus Christ patterns our submission to earthly authority.

"Submit" is what a servant or bondservant does for his master. In the New Testament, the Greek word is *doulos*. It means you give yourself up to another's will for the purpose of advancing a cause. It requires devotion—a disregard of your own interests. Submission means we consciously choose to trust those placed in authority over us.

Submission is seldom easy—but it's always necessary. This week, we'll be learning how to develop a servant's heart so that we're able to obey and to submit. If we truly understand our role as a *doulos* Christian, our role as a *doulos* athlete will be transformed.

Team Truth: *Submit yourselves, then, to God.* (James 4:7a)

Team Time: Let's start this week's Team Time with something easy. List three practical ways an athlete can demonstrate submission.

1.____

2.____

3. ____

Week 2: Surrendering to Submission, Day 2

It's more than swinging a racket

Michael was a talented young athlete. Straight A's combined with agility and solid ground strokes made the teen a serious challenger in the classroom and on the tennis court. His only trouble was an erupting temper as quick as his footwork. Rackets and words flew fast, balls sailed over the fence in frustration, and matches ended quickly.

Enter a new coach, David DeLancey: owner of a 101-0 college record, a touring tennis professional, USN Captain and fighter pilot, Special Operations Field Commander, and now a ranked seniors player and sought-after coach. He's affable and easygoing—until a player refuses to submit. He doesn't yell and scream, but he does demand compliance.

Things weren't going well on the court between Michael and his coach. Michael was undisciplined—he lacked concentration and exerted minimal effort.

"Michael, this is unacceptable. You'll run a lap every time you miss a shot. You'll go harder, work longer when you lose control. If you don't fix it, that's fine, but I'm gone. Find another coach. This is my tennis court and you'll play my way."

Michael had to make a decision.

He decided to submit. He didn't always like it, but he learned that his coach did know best. His tennis game improved radically, taking him all the way to the state finals.

But Michael's submission wasn't limited to the courts. His father, a traditional Chinese gentleman, was so impressed with the changes that he considered the coach a "Master." More than a teacher, a master assumes a definitive role in the development of the whole person. In gratitude, the father made DeLancey an honorary member of the family. He continues to train Michael on and off the court.

Have you ever been under the heavy hand of a coach, cursing under your breath as he pushed you to new limits? You might have thought, *I can't take this anymore*. But if you stuck with it, submitting to the coach's demands, you probably saw great improvement.

Submission demands that we trust the one in charge to know and do what's right. We can certainly trust God along those lines. As Christian athletes, we may not fully understand our athletic coach, but our role is to accept his authority because we have willingly placed ourselves under his care.

Team Truth: *Have confidence in your leaders and submit to their authority, because they keep watch over you as those who must give an account. Do this so that their work will be a joy, not a burden, for that would be of no benefit to you.* (Hebrews 13:17)

Team Time: Identify a time when you did not submit to your coach. What happened after that? How can you keep that from happening again?

____

____

____

____

____

____

____

____

Week 2: Surrendering to Submission, Day 3

A matter of conscience

Third and goal to go in the fourth quarter. The crowd rose to its feet, watching the drama unfold. The Trojans could topple the division powerhouse if they could only get the ball over the goal line. With scant seconds left on the clock, the coach called the last timeout of the game. Todd, a gifted quarterback who had drawn a number of college scouts to the game, listened as his coach handed him the play and then ran back onto the field. It was now or never.

Huddled together, the players heard the plan and executed it perfectly. A deafening cheer rose from the stands as the receiver pulled the ball into his chest for a touchdown. All was well. Or was it?

"Todd, get over here," the bewildered coach hollered over the roar. An onlooker might have been surprised that the coach didn't seem all that pleased with the win. The quarterback sauntered over, expecting congratulations. Instead he heard this: "What in the world were you thinking? I told you explicitly to run a ground play and you went to the air. Who do you think you are to defy me?"

"But Coach, we won when no one thought we could! I knew I could make my play work." With that, the coach shook his head and turned away. Oblivious to the celebration around him, he made a lonely walk back into the locker room. Todd, on the other hand, simply shrugged his shoulders and rejoined the merriment.

Are we to be pragmatic in this case? Was Todd right to run his own play and abandon the coach's instructions? Because Todd's plan worked out okay, does that justify defying the coach?

The apostle Paul wrote a letter to the Romans, an established church comprised of converted Jews and Gentiles, both free and slaves. Living in Rome in that era (circa AD 60) was no picnic. Nero, the emperor, entertained himself and Rome's citizens by persecuting Christians, reportedly burning them alive in his gardens to light the night. It's no wonder the church rebelled at the prospect of pledging allegiance and paying taxes to the evil leader and his government.

Nevertheless, Paul addressed the necessity of submitting to authority on two counts: to avoid punishment and to maintain a clear conscience. That is, do it because it's the right thing to do. Uh-oh! Submission in the light of horrific conditions goes against human nature. But Paul makes a compelling case: submission, regardless of the situation, is necessary if we are to be considered righteous by God.

Team Truth: *For the one in authority is God's servant for your good . . . Therefore, it is necessary to submit to the authorities, not only because of possible punishment but also as a matter of conscience.* (Romans 13: 4-5)

Team Time: Sooner or later, an athlete will disagree with a coach. How should a Christian athlete handle that? Is there a right time/way to discuss disagreements?

____

____

____

____

____

____

____

____

____

____

Week 2: Surrendering to Submission, Day 4

Submission even when it hurts

Imagine. You're an early first century man and have been chosen as high priest—a huge privilege because you make sacrifices to atone for the people's sins. But now, one man of Bethlehem birth, Jesus, is claiming to be God's Son. Some say He's reported to be the ultimate high priest, offering His own life as the definitive sacrifice for sin. You might lose your job because of this new guy.

Was Jesus stoked to move into that important position? Hardly. Consider this. Jesus Christ knew ahead of time that taking on the sin of the world would be agonizing. No one in his right mind would look forward to torture and death by crucifixion, not even Jesus Christ. So what did He do? "During the days of Jesus' life on earth, he offered up prayers and petitions with fervent cries and tears to the one who could save him from death, and he was heard because of his reverent submission" (Hebrews 5:7). It sounds as if this prayer was constantly on His heart and in His mind.

But please notice that Jesus, the Messiah, didn't necessarily suffer in silence. He voiced His concerns to the only one who had the power to change the course of history: God, His Father. Jesus' prayer was neither demanding nor obnoxious. Rather, He was simply having honest conversations with His Father.

Let's read verse seven again. "During the days of Jesus' life on earth, he offered up prayers and petitions with fervent cries and tears to the one who could save him from death, and he was heard because of his reverent submission." God heard and acknowledged the prayers of His Son because of "reverent submission." But did the fact that God listened to His Son mean Jesus avoided what was to come?

No. It did not. "Son though he was, he learned obedience from what he suffered and, once made perfect, he became the source of eternal salvation for all who obey him" (Hebrews 5:8b-9).

Ah. Suffering was part of the plan. That's why God listened but did not change His mind or course of action. A gigantic pill to swallow—even for Jesus.

We can be sure that God will hear our prayers and pleas if we voice them in a spirit of submission. However, we shouldn't be surprised if God chooses not to deliver us. Through reverent submission, we learn to be obedient and to be content with the outcome—two difficult lessons, but ones that are well worth learning.

Team Truth: *And he was heard because of his reverent submission.* (Hebrews 5:7b)

Team Time: Should a coach allow dissenting opinions to surface? How should an athlete react if the coach doesn't do what his player wants?

Week 2: Surrendering to Submission, Day 5

I think my coach is trying to kill me

Joy, Megan, and Piper glanced at each other through sweat-clouded eyes. None of them were enjoying this moment. Doubled over with their hands on knees, their chests heaved as they gasped for breath. Piper gagged, wrenching when her lunch tried to escape. But the ordeal wasn't over.

"Back on the line. Let's go again. Now!" Coach Treborne barked. He demanded immediate action. Still not recovered, the three girls stood upright and scurried to the line. They'd seen teammates thrown out of practice and confined to the sidelines for not moving fast enough. Coach bellowed, "You have three more suicides coming your way. First group. Go!" Trying to ignore their quivering muscles, the trio raced down the field. More pain. More agony.

Just like athletes, coaches come in all shapes and sizes, with personalities just as varied. Some are easygoing. Others make a habit of screaming and scowling like a Marine drill instructor. They may even be insulting and demeaning. How should the Christian athlete respond?

The book of 1 Peter was likely written around AD 62. Peter directed the letter to Christian converts in Pontus, Galatia, Cappadocia, Asia, and Bithynia. The long arm of the Roman Empire stretched to these areas and Christ-followers endured intense persecution. Peter used their situation to teach several important concepts.

First, he tells them to submit to every human authority. He also tells the slaves to respect their masters even when they are evil. Peter follows that by saying wives need to submit to unbelieving husbands. Hardly seems fair, does it?

Why did Peter give instructions that go against human nature? It all comes down to this: "Live such good lives among the pagans that, though they accuse you of doing wrong, they may see your good deeds and glorify God . . . For it is commendable if someone bears up under the pain of unjust suffering because they are conscious of God" (1 Peter 2:12, 19).

Although we're not slaves, our coach might make us feel that way. Sure, it's tough to stomach strict rules and horrendous practices. And yes, the coach should be a good and fair leader. But when we place ourselves on a team and under the coach's authority, we must choose to submit because we are "conscious of God."

Team Truth: *For it is God's will that by doing good you should silence the ignorant talk of foolish people.* (1 Peter 2:15)

Team Time: Let's be honest, some coaches are mean and harsh. They may lack knowledge, and they may push athletes beyond what is safe. Does your responsibility to submit change under these circumstances? Is there a time to say "no"? Should you quit if you can't (or won't) submit?

Week 3: Motivation Meets Aspiration, Day 1

The hooked fish

It was one of the funniest things she'd ever seen. A young boy, perhaps five years old, was fishing with his father. He held one of those flimsy kid-sized poles. His inadequate equipment and childish impatience suggested that he wasn't going to catch anything. Miraculously, when he yanked up on the pole for the umpteenth time, a fish dangled from the end. Wiggling almost as much as the hooked fish, the delighted boy scampered along the bank, extending his arm as he attempted to grab the fish. Though he tried and tried, wrapping his little fingers around that fish was impossible because he continued to hold the tip of his pole just out of reach. No matter how hard he tried, he was chasing an unobtainable goal; he never drew closer despite his constant running. Success meant one of two things: either the boy had to change his method or the goal had to be redefined.

Intuitively, we know that pursuing a goal draws us forward. But just like the little boy, if the goal is always out of reach, we'll probably quit along the way out of pure exhaustion.

The Bible talks specifically about goals in several places. Even Jesus set goals for Himself. Surprised? Here's what happened.

In chapter thirteen of his book, Dr. Luke describes several of Jesus' ministry experiences: a parable about the fig tree, a mustard seed, and a narrow door. He recounts how Jesus healed a crippled woman. But then, he tells a story about those self-righteous Pharisees who tried to trick Jesus into diverting His trip away from Jerusalem.

The Pharisees, religious rulers in New Testament times, weren't very excited that some guy was performing miracles and claiming to be God's Son. If He was right, many people would follow Him and that would strip away the Pharisees' power and prestige. In this encounter, they tried to sweet-talk Jesus, pretending to be concerned over His well-being. They said, "'Leave this place and go somewhere else. Herod wants to kill you'" (Luke 13:31). But Jesus wasn't fooled.

Jesus countered them specifically. And He didn't take any guff. In fact, He said, "Go tell that fox, 'I will keep on driving out demons and healing people today and tomorrow, and on the third day I will reach my goal.' In any case, I must press on today and tomorrow and the next day" (Luke 13:32-33).

What's the lesson for us? Jesus knew what needed to be accomplished and formulated a specific plan. Please note that He wasn't making a plan for three years down the road; He'd set a goal for the next three days. He spoke boldly because He knew exactly what He needed to do and when He needed to do it. We should be so wise.

Team Truth: *"In any case, I must press on today and tomorrow and the next day."* (Luke 13:33a)

Team Time: Short-term plans are as important as long-term goals. Given your upcoming schedule, define what you need to do (as a team or individually) in the next three days of training. Develop a habit of making intentional, specific short-term plans.

____

____

____

____

____

____

____

Week 3: Motivation Meets Aspiration, Day 2

Past blasts don't count

He was so good. Incredibly talented. Steve seemed to have it all. There wasn't anything he couldn't do. When he was six, his pee-wee football team couldn't score without him. The Little League Tigers counted on his fast ball to strike out would-be hitters. And all through middle school and the early years of high school, this year-round athlete racked up one award after another for his play on the field, the court, and the track.

In his senior year, Steve was captain of all his teams, seeing more playing time than anyone else. But something was different. He had the same skills but not the same attitude. No excitement, no enthusiasm. Maybe he was tired. Burnt out. Or the emotionless eyes could mean Steve was content to live off past performances. He'd always been special and he knew it. Why not take it easy and rest on his laurels? He'd earned that privilege, hadn't he?

Then there was Paul. Born into a wealthy family, Paul had all the advantages of a privileged life. He was a very special kind of Hebrew: he belonged to the tribe of Benjamin and he'd been circumcised on cue. He'd been given the best education money could buy and the credentials to prove it. Paul could recite the Law backwards, forwards, and upside down. If righteousness depended on these things, he was as righteous a Pharisee as they came—faultless, even.

The problem was this: when Paul came to know Christ in an up-close-and-personal way, he realized all his prior accomplishments meant nothing. In fact, he considered them "garbage" (Philippians 3:8). Paul's recognition of his unrighteousness in the light of Christ's righteousness redirected his thinking. He wanted nothing more than "to know Christ—yes, to know the power of his resurrection" (v. 10). But did that happen without purposeful intent? It doesn't look that way.

Paul says, "Not that I have already obtained all this, or have already arrived at my goal, but I press on to take hold of that for which Christ Jesus took hold of me . . . But one thing I do: Forgetting what is behind and straining toward what is ahead, I press on toward the goal to win the prize for which God has called me heavenward in Christ Jesus" (Philippians 3:12-14).

It really doesn't matter what we've done in the past. What counts is that we look to the future. We strive to make forward progress. In verse 15, Paul says that mature Christians understand that the goal of righteousness should dictate how we play out our lives. That's much more important than scoring double digits in a basketball game. Rather, our goal in everything we do—athletics, academics, interpersonal relationships—should be to become more like Christ.

Team Truth: *I press on to take hold of that for which Christ Jesus took hold of me.* (Philippians 3:12b)

Team Time: Specifically, how can your sport be an opportunity to become "righteousness"—to do what is right? Give examples of how that might look at practice or at a competition.

1.____

2. _______________________________________

3. _______________________________________

4. _______________________________________

5. _______________________________________

6. _______________________________________

7. _______________________________________

8. _______________________________________

Week 3: Motivation Meets Aspiration, Day 3

Trustworthy to tumble

Right at five feet tall, Taylor carried an explosive charge in a tiny package. An elite gymnast, her tumbling passes wowed the crowd. She catapulted her frame through the air, twisting and flipping more times than should be humanly possible. She made it look so easy.

But it wasn't easy. Each morning she arose before roosters even thought about crowing. Breakfast, training, school work, more training, lunch, training all afternoon, supper, review performance tapes, complete school work, and fall into bed for a few hours. Her dream to compete on an Olympic stage drove her to repeat the process day after day, year after year. Her public platform awaited her. Or did it?

Like Taylor, we're all motivated by huge golden carrots hung in front of us. The Olympics, world championships, or even the hope of winning seasons and conference titles can coax out the best in us. All good stuff. But we might be missing many opportunities if that's all that drives us toward our goals.

The apostle Paul wrote to Timothy and the Ephesian

church about losing focus. It seems the Ephesians habitually argued about details of the law, and they tangled themselves in busyness, rather than focusing on what was much more important: advancing God's work. Not that the law was worthless. In fact, Paul says, "We know that the law is good if one uses it properly" (1 Timothy 1:5). But the Ephesians lost focus because they got so hung up in themselves. Don't be too critical, though. Losing focus is easy.

Paul instructed Timothy to remind the Ephesians of the overriding goal: "[to] love, which comes from a pure heart and a good conscience and a sincere faith" (1 Timothy 1:5). But how does that apply to Taylor? To us as athletes?

To unlock the mystery we must understand that we are athletes by God's express intention. As athletes, we have access to people and situations otherwise alien. Trouble comes when we get lost in our training and the pursuit of tangible goals. Then we fail to make the most of every opportunity to do what God commands: love out of a pure heart, good conscience, and a sincere faith.

So, is Taylor wrong to aggressively pursue her dreams of an Olympic venue? She could give testimony once she dismounts the uneven bars, climbs the awards podium, and is interviewed on national television, right? Right. But Taylor needs to understand, as do we, that every training session, every encounter with her coach, teammates, and competitors is an opportunity to love in very practical ways. Taylor will minister within her athletic pursuits if, like Paul, she testifies,

"I thank Christ Jesus our Lord, who has given me strength, that he considered me trustworthy, appointing me to his service" (1 Timothy 1:12).

Team Truth: *The goal of this command is love, which comes from a pure heart and a good conscience and a sincere faith.* (1 Timothy 1:5)

Team Time: We serve God through athletics and we are commanded to love (v. 5). Practically, how do we do that? Give specific examples.

____

____

____

____

____

____

____

____

____

Week 3: Motivation Meets Aspiration, Day 4

Refuse to lose

On a warm spring day in 1976, David DeLancey stepped onto the tennis court for the third set of a college match. DeLancey had been aggressively recruited to play soccer for Cedarville College in 1972, but at that time was unknown for his tennis skills. Still, as a walk-on, he immediately earned the number one position on the tennis team. Against all odds, he accrued a perfect record of ninety-one wins and zero loses. But on that particular day in May, it looked like his stellar streak would end.

With a heavy topspin on both his forehand and backhand, DeLancey's opponent from Ohio Northern University was proving problematic. They split the first two sets. In the third and final set, hope was fading fast when the Cedarville senior went down five games to nil. Just four points stood in the way of an upset of gigantic proportions.

DeLancey, silently suffering his senior year from migraines brought on by the pressure of his perfect record, had a plan. He had no time for fear or speculation about losing. No. He had but one objective: make every point count.

In peak athletic condition, DeLancey followed every serve and service return to the net. The undefeated player's attack was furious and unrelenting. His opponent's nerves began to unravel. DeLancey's ruthless net play turned the set score to 5-1. As he focused only on one point at a time, the scorecards flipped to 5-2, then 5-3. Fans and teammates witnessed the amazing comeback. Without a single deuce game, DeLancey handily won seven games straight to win both the set and match. His record remained unsoiled, setting the stage to round out his college career with an unprecedented 101-0 record.

What was the key to his success? Was it his technically correct strokes or his outstanding fitness level? Sure, that was part of it. But his primary motivation wasn't to win; he was committed to do whatever it took *not* to lose. That meant shutting out the past and the future so he could focus only on the moment.

It all boils down to what happens in a single instant. The centurion's servant was healed in a moment. Remember the sick woman who strained to touch the hem of Jesus' robe? "'Take heart, daughter,' he said, 'your faith has healed you.' And the woman was healed at that moment" (Matthew 9:23). But the greatest single moment? The very instant Christ's death on the cross made our salvation possible.

Team Truth: *And when Jesus had cried out again in a loud voice, he gave up his spirit. At that moment the curtain of the temple was torn in two from top to bottom.* (Matthew 27: 50-51a)

Team Time: Have you ever been "in the moment"? What was it like? How can you consistently compete "in the moment"?

____

____

____

____

____

____

____

____

____

____

Week 3: Motivation Meets Aspiration, Day 5

A funny thing happened on the way

The goal? Defeat Midian, a heathen nation that relentlessly attacked, pillaged, and made life miserable for the Israelites.

Put yourself in Gideon's sandals, the reluctant leader who whispered to God, "'Pardon me, my lord . . . but how can I save Israel? My clan is the weakest . . . and I am the least in my family'" (Judges 6:15). In a series of up-close-and-personals, God convinced Gideon to embrace the goal of attacking his nasty neighbors. But that doesn't mean he was convinced of what it would take to do so.

His first God-assignment was tearing down the altar to Baal, but Gideon was a reluctant warrior. He did the deed at night because he feared that people would be angry and kill him. He was right. They were angry and wanted revenge. Only after God gave him two sure signs did Gideon actually believe God would protect him.

Gathering an army was his next task—easier said than done without email and Facebook. Still, thirty-two thousand guys showed up. Gideon rejoiced—until God told him that he had too many men. If they fought with that number, they might think the victory was theirs and not God's. Heavy sigh. Gideon announced that anyone who was afraid could go home. Twenty-two thousand men beat feet.

Ten thousand guys remained. Gideon led them to water and instructed them to drink. Most put their faces to the water. They got pink slips and headed home as well. By the time God's training classes ended, Gideon's army was only three hundred strong. He must have wondered how the goal could be achieved with so few.

He asked God for another sign and got it. He sneaked into the Midianite camp and overheard one soldier tell another of a nightmare he'd just had: they were about to be whooped. Gideon was back on track. He divided the men into three groups of one hundred each, arming them only with a trumpet in one hand and a jar covering a candle in the other. Not one machine gun or automatic rifle. Not even a lousy sword! Positioned around the camp, the Israelites blew their trumpets when they broke the jars, scaring the bejeebers out of the Midianites. In fact, they became so disoriented by Gideon's strange "attack" that they turned their own swords on each other. Not one Midianite was left standing. Goal achieved and victory claimed. Who could've predicted that?

We can pigeonhole ourselves by thinking only one road leads to our goal. But if Gideon's story is any indication, we shouldn't be surprised when God presents another path. Gideon had questions. Twice he said, "Pardon me, my Lord, but . . ." Two times he watched his army shrink. Three times he asked for special signs. The road to victory was convoluted. Gideon could only see one turn at a time, but he was traveling the right road. He just needed to trust the road builder.

Team Truth: *The LORD turned to him and said, "Go . . . Am I not sending you?"* (Judges 6:14)

Team Time: Have you met a goal in an unexpected way? Describe what happened.

____

____

____

____

____

____

____

____

____

Week 4: Fear and Dreams, Day 1

When fear and dreams collide

Picture this: You're poised to leave your family and fly to another continent and into the unknown. You'll race on foot through the harsh Brazilian jungle for seven days, covering 250 kilometers. Everything that you need will be on your back when you start. No one will provide food or transport your gear. The only aid you'll receive is an occasional bottle of sun-warmed water.

You've never done anything like this. You don't know what to take or how to survive in a rotting, sodden jungle. What about snakes, leeches, piranhas, and jaguars? What about blisters on your feet and poisonous thorns on trees? What if you can't make the required distance each day? What if you have to drop out in shame?

The fear is real. Rebekah Trittipoe knows. She was there. She lived through dehydration and potentially fatal sickness. She put one foot in front of the other even when she thought it might be her last step. But one night, as she stood in the middle of the trail and peered into the night sky, the infinite number of stars reminded her that the God who made each one watched over her. In that defining moment, Rebekah realized that her hopes and dreams had overcome her fear.

She's not the only one who has experienced that. Consider Moses. After wandering around a giant sandbox for forty years, he looked into Canaan, the Promised Land. It was filled with giants who were more than willing to protect their land. Ten spies, sent to scope out the situation, reported that conquering those giants was impossible. "No way. We'll be squashed like bugs," they said. But two other spies, Joshua and Caleb, refused to think that way. They experienced victory because they clung to hope despite their fear.

Or what about a young girl, Mary, who discovered she was pregnant? She wasn't married. She'd never had sex, but who'd believe her? What would the cranky old lady down the street say about her? How could she live with all the trash talk circling her? The Bible says Mary was "greatly troubled. But the angel said to her, 'Do not be afraid, Mary; you have found favor with God'" (Luke 1:29-30). Mary didn't have to live in fear. God gave her hope.

God understands that we struggle with fear. But He also promises that if we fully trust Him, fear will fall in defeat, and hope and dreams will soar in victory.

Team Truth: *Be strong and courageous. Do not be afraid or terrified because of them, for the LORD your God goes with you; he will never leave you nor forsake you.* (Deuteronomy 31:6)

Team Time: Let's talk about the fear we have as individuals. List three specific things you fear about this season.

1. ____
2. ____
3. ____

Week 4: Fear and Dreams, Day 2

Teetering and terrified

In 2006, a Georgia church decided to produce a movie with a message. With a budget of $100,000 (microscopic by Hollywood standards), the film broke into the public sector, grossing an amazing $20 million at the box office. It was called *Facing the Giants.*

Here's the synopsis: Against all odds, a Christian school's football team, which had a losing record, ends up taking the state title. Through the course of the story, the coach, his wife, and members of the team experience a revival of sorts, understanding what it means to give God everything. Despite its predictability, the motivational movie's undeniably authentic message is clear and bold.

One memorable moment in the movie stands out. In an empty, dimly lit locker room the pensive coach awaits the arrival of his players. The proverbial calm before the storm. Enter the coach's own boyhood coach. During the exchange of well wishes, the facts of the ensuing battle arise. The opposing team has three times as many players, has been state champs for several years, and is physically powerful and enormous. They are the "giants" and the little "Davids" are barely able to nip at their heels. In order to win the battle on the football field, the "Davids" would first have to conquer their fear. The wise old coach offers: "God says in His Word, 'Do not fear,' 365 times. So, go out there and play" (paraphrased)* .

Three hundred sixty-five times. Wow! That amounts to one "do not fear" for every day of the year. As always, God is sufficient for every situation, every day. In the Bible, people are afraid for many reasons: opposing armies, cruel captors, hoards of bugs, death, evil people, a storm on the seas, or the dark night. We have reasons to be fearful as well. We fear we'll lose a championship, drop a fly ball that lets the winning run score, be embarrassed, flunk a test, disappoint our parents, or lose all our friends. Still, we can be fearless even in the most terrifying circumstances. As Jesus told the synagogue ruler, "Don't be afraid; just believe" (Mark 5:36).

Team Truth: *Moses answered the people, "Do not be afraid. Stand firm and you will see the deliverance the LORD will bring you today."* (Exodus 14:13)

Team Time: Fill in the following sentence as it applies to you. My biggest fear concerning my role on this team is:

I can address this fear by:

**Facing the Giants.* Directed by Alex Kendrick. 111 minutes. Samuel Goldwyn Films. 2006.

Week 4: Fear and Dreams, Day 3

I'm a big, fat loser

Ever hear of the Bad News Bears?* You may remember the story of the misfit kids who ended up on a baseball team. Fat kids, skinny kids, weird kids, a motorcycling punk, and a girl, of all things. Their coach was a crude, rude, out-of-shape, beer-guzzling ex-minor-leaguer-turned-pool-cleaner. He consented, for money, to coach the town's Little League team. Except for the punk and the girl, the lineup had little talent and poor team dynamics. As happens so often in movies, the team members mysteriously gelled, discovered a common goal, rose to heights previously unknown, and knocked off their arch nemesis in the championship game. Hardly realistic. But the story works because we like to cheer for the underdogs.

A similar thing happened in the Bible. Another team of misfits formed in a dark, damp cave.

David, son of Jesse, was fleeing from King Saul. He'd sharpened his royal spear hoping to make a shish kabob of David's heart. David had to run all over the countryside to avoid the jealous king. He fled from his Gath hideout to hole up in a cave in Adullam. But he wasn't alone. Curious parties showed up to check out David's situation. However, these men weren't exactly the most stellar members of society. Rather, the Bible says, "All those who were in distress or in debt or discontented gathered around him, and he became their leader" (1 Samuel 22:2). Delinquents, misfits, and malcontents—four hundred men strong.

Can you believe those guys became the strongest, most victorious army of that era? They didn't succeed because they were huge, bulky men and highly trained soldiers. No. They were just guys who didn't fit in. King David took that straggly bunch and conquered the kingdom with them because they were willing participants in God's ordained plan.

Don't fret about your imperfections. Don't worry about feeling inferior. Don't think you're a loser. Don't focus on what you lack. Focus on what you have that makes you special. Remember, it's not "you" that makes the difference. It's God working through you that produces results.

Team Truth: *"Not by might nor by power, but by my Spirit," says the LORD Almighty.* (Zechariah 4:6b)

Team Time: Let's be honest. Most of us feel inadequate in some way. What's the one thing that most often makes you feel inferior? Admitting it is the first step to conquering it.

____

____

____

____

____

____

____

____

____

____

____

____

**Bad News Bears*. Directed by Michael Ritchie. 113 minutes. Paramount Pictures. 1976.

Week 4: Fear and Dreams, Day 4

Fearful fumbling

Fear is an interesting emotion. Powerful chemicals rampage through our bodies. We feel our heart race as our core heats up. Our palms sweat; our breathing becomes faster, shallower. And we can't seem to keep our muscles from twitching in anticipation of things to come. Sometimes, even our stomachs lurch and send us racing to the nearest bathroom to lighten the load. Fear is not a pleasant sensation.

So, why is fear so powerful, so invasive? Can we—or should we—suppress fear? Good questions. Let's look at an example.

Bottom of the ninth. The Knights trail 3-4 in the state championships. Runners on first and second. Two outs. Freddy waits at the plate for his first pitch. For the first time in the school's history, the team has made it this far in post-season play. The stands are packed, fans roaring like hungry lions in pursuit of their prey. Freddy isn't feeling too good. He tries to control the trembling and slow his breathing. He hears his heart pounding in his head. His wild eyes steal quick glances down the lines and out to the farthest fence. He hopes the bat won't slip from his sweaty palms. How he wishes he could be standing anywhere but in the batter's box. The future of the entire human race rests upon his shoulders—at least that's how he feels.

What's going on here? Freddy might be fearful because of the disappointment he could cause an entire town should he strike out or hit an easy pop fly to shortstop. *They'll all hate me for losing this game,* he figures. *I can see the headlines now: Freddie's Strikeout Kills Championship Dream.*

Or he may be fearful because it's his last chance to prove to the coach that he really is superior to Tom, the guy he replaced in the starting lineup. Better yet, Freddy really needs to hit one out of the park to impress the college scout watching from the stands. What he does with this at-bat might alter the course of his future. What pressure!

We could glibly state that God is not the god of fear—which is true—before preaching that we should never feel fearful. But that's too easy. God knows we fear and has given us principles to control it. In fact, fear subsides when we gain perspective.

Putting aside unrealistic expectations, refusing to worry about what someone else thinks, and discarding unattainable perfectionism will help us to hold fear at bay. Relax. Trust your training. Ask God to provide the focus. Do your best and be content with the outcome.

Team Truth: *For God hath not given us the spirit of fear; but of power, and of love, and of a sound mind.* (2 Timothy 1:7 KJV)

Team Time: Fear is a real emotion. What can you do to control fear in high pressure situations? How can you help a teammate who is terrified of performing poorly? Think in practical terms.

Week 4: Fear and Dreams, Day 5

Oh, so scared

Imagine this. You're in peak physical condition, part of the reason you were selected to fly jets in the US Navy. So far, you've logged a mere two hundred air hours, only about a quarter of those in an actual jet. Now the order comes: land on an aircraft carrier bobbing around in the ocean. Your flight instructor's plane is grounded, so you must fly alone in your single-seat fighter. Soaring at breakneck speed, the blue ocean beneath your wings, you gasp when you first see the USS Lexington. Your heart beats wildly. You must reign in your emotions.

Even at 910 feet in length, the carrier looks more like a bathtub toy from your vantage point. The ship moves forward and to the left. It generates its own wind and creates dangerous vacuums and air currents that can suck your plane down one minute and in the next instant thrust it heavenward. The carrier rocks and rolls in the waves, listing twelve degrees to the left. All the pilots in this fleet of planes, you being one of them, are seeing a carrier for the first time. Each pilot will land his jet in forty-five second intervals, coming in at full throttle in case the plane's hook fails to catch the wire strung low across the deck. It's life and death, literally, at regular intervals.

You feel the pull of seven Gs as you drop "into the break" at six hundred feet above the surface. Now the signal comes. You make the last of the complicated maneuvers to drop farther to three hundred feet. Your eyes frantically search for the Fresnel lens and the guiding lights that you can only see when your plane is properly aligned. But you are chasing a listing, moving target. Only eleven vertical feet stand between a perfect landing and death: eleven feet too low and your plane smashes into the back of the ship. Perfection is your only option.

You take a deep breath as you close in on the ship. Your hook catches, engines still at full throttle. Your body violently decelerates from 140 mph to zero in a split second. The deck hands rush to pull your plane aside and secure it before the next plane puts its wheels on deck. You've survived the first landing despite your fear. Soon they catapult you back into the air to face the fear again. And again. And again.

Applying what he knew to be true and discerning what was most important each moment were the key factors in the pilot's success. Though his fear was keen before and after the landing, he conquered that potentially fatal fear with discernment and focus.

Team Truth: *A discerning person keeps wisdom in view, but a fool's eyes wander to the ends of the earth.* (Proverbs 17:24)

Team Time: How can knowledge and discernment help you conquer fear in the athletic arena? Give a couple of specific, practical examples.

____

____

____

____

____

____

____

____

____

Week 5: Yowza. This Hurts Bad! Day 1

Broken, but persistent

It was her first fifty-mile race through the mountains. In the early morning chill, she ran the first seven miles on pure adrenalin. But as the miles of rocky trail, steep climbs, and soaking stream-crossings piled up, her endorphin levels plummeted. She was left with an increasing level of awareness: calves growing tighter; quads struggling to power up the mountains; the mental anguish of chasing down the lead runner while being chased from behind; exhausted chest muscles unaccustomed to such forced and frequent breathing.

Her husband waited for her at mile thirty-seven with fresh bottles of water and her favorite snacks. But just as they made the exchange, Rebekah stepped awkwardly on a rock. She screeched as her ankle twisted pretzel-like. Her vision went black, head spinning. She wanted to throw up. In a flash, the ankle morphed into something unrecognizable—big as a strongman's biceps and a sickening shade of blue. Pain, like searing spikes, shot upward when she tried to take a step. Tears ran hot, stinging her cheeks. How could she go on?

The general consensus? Her ankle was fractured. Most

runners would've called it a day. Rebekah chose to continue. Every step of the remaining thirteen tortuous miles was agony. She knew that she couldn't take the lead, but the thought of being passed this late in the race drove her up, down, and around those mountains, alternately whimpering and wailing. An endless stream of tears watered each foot plant. By the time she saw the finish line, the discoloration had risen to her knee and her ankle was enormous. Still, she passed under the banner. She had withstood the suffering and anguish of the last few hours—hours that proved vital to her development as an extreme athlete.

No story is more motivating than that of the athlete who rises from the ashes in pursuit of glorious victory. Enduring—and overcoming—suffering matures us and puts things in perspective. But it sure would be easier if suffering didn't hurt so much.

Why suffer? We suffer because some things can only be learned the hard way. The apostle Paul said as much to the church in Rome. Those Christians endured emotional scorn and horrible torture because of their affiliation with Christ. Who yearned to be ripped apart by hungry lions, whipped senseless, or burned alive? No one. Yet Paul, speaking from his own experience, advised them to "glory" in their suffering because it leads to perseverance, which builds character, which leads to hope.

Just as there's no shortcut to fitness, there's no shortcut to hope. We must suffer first.

Team Truth: *Not only so, but we also glory in our sufferings, because we know that suffering produces perseverance; perseverance, character; and character, hope.* (Romans 5:3-4)

Team Time: Can perseverance be learned without suffering first? Why or why not? Give an example to support your answer.

____

____

____

____

____

____

____

____

____

Week 5: Yowza. This Hurts Bad! Day 2

This is gonna hurt

Sometimes suffering is inevitable. Sometimes it's a choice.

Ultrarunners choose to suffer every time they step to the starting line of a long race. They know it's going to hurt. They just don't know how badly.

Whether it's a race, a lacrosse game, or a tennis match, your all-out effort may shove you to the brink of your physical limits. Or the mental pressure may be so unsettling that your stomach revolts in violent protest: you puke. But you must press on. You must choose to suffer.

Thinking about an upcoming 100-mile race, the athlete knows what's coming. In the first few hours, he'll settle in, trying to face the long path ahead. Somewhere along the way, his foot will begin to hurt or a painful blister will develop. He'll fight a constant battle to take in—and keep down—sufficient calories and fluid. His eyes will droop from sleep deprivation, his quads rebelling while his back throbs with pain. Yet, despite knowing what lies ahead, he'll start when the gun sounds, running toward the place where the trail intersects with suffering's lonely path.

If he knows he's going to suffer, why does he voluntarily choose to do so? He chooses to suffer because it will be worth it in the end. Enduring indescribable fatigue and pain, he'll cross the finish line, triumphant.

Think about those who chose to suffer for more noble reasons than finishing a trail race. Paul and Barnabas traveled together, preaching and teaching in Iconium. Though many Jews believed, some weren't convinced of the gospel and rallied the Gentiles. They plotted to kill Barnabas and Paul, but undeterred, the two men simply left to preach in nearby Lystra. When they healed a lame man, the crowd misunderstood their power. Thinking they were actually the gods Zeus and Hermes, the people bowed and prepared to offer pagan sacrifices to them. Of course, Paul and Barnabas protested, proclaiming they were mere men, servants of the true God. But unbelieving Jews from Antioch and Iconium, seeking to entrap the men, rallied the crowd. Paul was dragged from the city, stoned, and left for dead.

Most people—if they survived—would take that as a sign never to return. Not Paul. He ventured back into the city, bruised and bleeding. The next day Paul and Barnabas traveled to Derbe to preach, but soon they returned to Lystra, the place of Paul's intense suffering. They couldn't keep a good man down.

Why? He had placed his hope in the future and in God's coming kingdom.

Team Truth: *Then they returned to Lystra, Iconium and Antioch, strengthening the disciples and encouraging them to remain true to the faith. "We must go through many hardships to enter the kingdom of God," they said.* (Acts 14:21b-22)

Team Time: If you're an athlete, you will suffer. Sometimes we endure suffering better if we're not alone. How can you help your teammates endure—and embrace—inevitable suffering? Record a specific example.

Week 5: Yowza. This Hurts Bad! Day 3

Tough timeouts

Stephen, a freshman new to the school, had been running strongly enough to claim a top seven varsity spot on the cross-country team. Knee pain that he could no longer bear led him to a doctor, who ordered him to stop running for three weeks. His training came to a screeching halt.

Morgan, another new freshman, came full of promise. She, too, earned a spot on the varsity squad. But she ran with an awkward gait, caused by strange anatomy and muscle imbalances. She was handed a decree of "No Running" for six weeks.

Coach Trittipoe feels their pain. She's been there. In the first five years of ultrarunning, she suffered nine metatarsal fractures, medial malleolus and femoral neck fractures, a torn tibial aponeuroses, surgeries on both feet and an ankle (involving seven incisions and eight screws), along with multiple soft tissue injuries.

Like a tadpole, into the pool she went, deep-water running sometimes for three hours at a time to maintain fitness. Weeks later, she emerged with fresh legs to train like a madman, only to break something else. Back she went into the cold, deep pond of despair. An endless, maddening cycle. She wanted so much to be fit, racing fast and strong. But that wasn't God's plan. At least not for a while.

We do our best to be smart and avoid injury but unfortunately, pain and suffering may still come our way. It's frustrating and agonizing in so many ways—physically, emotionally, and sometimes even spiritually. Being a wounded warrior makes us feel less of an athlete, less of a contributor to the team. Sometimes, we think we've lost all connection with the team. But despite how we feel, these tough timeouts won't last forever.

Sitting on the sideline watching others train and compete is hard. We experience loneliness, inadequacies, and disappointment. We feel betrayed by our own bodies. Healing time moves more slowly than a glacier. The wait is excruciating.

But sometimes we need to wait. We must learn to wait, not in a vacuum, but in the healing atmosphere of expectant hope created by full submission to a loving God. We must put things in perspective and learn to be content. We need to make the most of our downtime so we'll be better prepared when we're off and running again. And patience often brings unexpected blessings: when we slow down, we may clearly spot things that we could never see when we were racing along at breakneck speed.

Sure, a timeout is unpleasant and unwelcome. But it isn't the end of the world. This too shall pass.

Team Truth: *Then your light will break forth like the dawn, and your healing will quickly appear; then your righteousness will go before you, and the glory of the LORD will be your rear guard.* (Isaiah 58:8)

Team Time: Someone on the team is probably injured right now. Identify specific ways you can encourage them and show them that they're still an integral part of the team.

1.______________________________

2.______________________________

3.______________________________

4.______________________________

5.______________________________

6.______________________________

7.______________________________

8.______________________________

Week 5: Yowza. This Hurts Bad! Day 4

Suffering 101

"I came to realize I wasn't very good at team sports. Look at me. I'm too small for football or basketball. But I found out I'm really good at suffering."

Scotty Curlee delivered those words to the Liberty Christian Academy track team. Every kid in the room was captivated with this professional cyclist turned leading actor and movie director (*The Potential Inside*). Curlee continued, "I was the guy who could peg the heart rate and crank it up Apple Orchard Mountain despite the pain, the rain, the cold . . . To race at the Olympic and world-class level, you must choose to sacrifice. You must choose to suffer."

Rick Gray, an experienced and vibrant ultrarunner, chose to suffer. With a goal of sub-twenty hours at the Umstead 100 Miler, he took step after relentless step. But somewhere between the start and the finish, his stomach turned south, forcing him to endure retching and heaving, the kind that reduces a body to mush. The last twenty-five mile trudge was nothing but slow, agonizing torture. Yet, he endured to the end despite missing his target time. He, too, chose to suffer.

Great feats of physical accomplishments are examples of perseverance through adversity. Such stories inspire and motivate—and make great movies. In fact, we tend to make new commitments and set lofty goals after seeing such tales. But alas, we fail to achieve those goals more often than not.

Why? Because suffering is hard—extremely, painfully, exceptionally hard. All the prior mental decisions vanish as the lactic acid accumulates, the legs begin to fail, and the heart feels like a time bomb ready to explode. The finish line is obscured by a blinding storm of pain and agony. Only the athlete who keeps a compelling and clear goal in sight claims the prize.

But there's another example of suffering no athlete comes close to topping. In this case, the suffering was endured because of the greatest commitment of all time—a commitment to suffer in the place of those who deserved punishment. This man chose to suffer for those who had no power to endure. In fact, they didn't even have the power to enter the game. Jesus Christ suffered on a cross two thousand years ago, providing a pathway to God the Father. Jesus' suffering was a necessary part of the Father's plan.

Team Truth: *[He] was despised and rejected by mankind, a man of suffering, and familiar with pain. Like one from whom people hide their faces he was despised, and we held him in low esteem. Surely he took up our pain and bore our suffering, yet we* *considered him punished by God, stricken by him, and afflicted. But he was pierced for our transgressions, he was crushed for our iniquities; the punishment that brought us peace was on him, and by his wounds we are healed.* (Isaiah 53:3-8)

Team Time: Identify a time when you flunked Suffering 101. Analyze why you chose to give up rather than endure the pain. How can you keep that from happening again?

____

____

____

____

____

____

____

____

Week 5: Yowza. This Hurts Bad! Day 5

Suffering feeds focus

On July 23, 1996, the eyes of the world were on Atlanta. The women's gymnastic event, always a crowd favorite, packed the Georgia Dome to capacity. Fans came to see the finals of the team competition. The home crowd roared its approval when the USA girls leaped, twirled, and tumbled their way into position to take the team gold medal. Ahead of the second place Russian team, all Team USA needed was a solid showing on the vault to earn gold. But when American vaulter, Dominique Moceanu, hit the mats on both her attempts, hope faded for the first-ever team title. Destiny lay on the tiny shoulders of Kerri Strug.

Just seventeen years old at the time, standing four feet nine inches and weighing a slight eighty-eight pounds, she needed to score 9.493 or better on the vault if the Magnificent Seven, as they were called, would take home gold. The crowd held its breath as she raced down the runway and launched into the air. On the landing, her feet slipped and she took a seat on the floor. Her parents—and the watching world—fell into shocked silence at the third straight fall by an American. The fact that she still could nail her second attempt kept hope alive. But when she rose, she limped badly back down the lane, her ankle injured.

Let's interrupt this story for a second. If you were Kerri, what would you be thinking? Can you imagine the barrage of thoughts swirling in your head? It would be hard not to crumple under the pressure and the expectations of teammates, coaches, parents, friends, onlookers, and most of all, self.

But let's go back to what happened. The injury itself brought everything into focus for Kerri. She chose to push away every thought of pain and of what might happen if she blew the next vault. She twisted through the air and stuck a perfect landing—on one leg—before collapsing to the mat. She had done it. Her score of 9.71 sealed the top spot for the Americans.

Pain grabs our attention. But we decide whether it will foil or focus us. In 1 Peter 4, the author tells us we should have the same attitude as Christ had when He suffered. He makes the point that when we suffer for Christ's sake, we're reminded that sin is behind us. Therefore, we focus on living for God and not evil. Without the pain, without the suffering, we'd likely forget our higher purpose.

Let's face it—suffering is never enjoyable. It hurts. It's a bother. Nevertheless, sometimes it's what we need to refocus on the objective.

Team Truth: *Therefore, since Christ suffered in his body, arm yourselves also with the same attitude, because whoever suffers in the body is done with sin. As a result, they do not live the rest of their earthly lives for evil human desires, but rather for the will of God.* (1 Peter 4:1-2)

Team Time: Describe a specific time when pain or suffering was exactly what you needed to refocus on the objective.

Week 6: Persevering Persistence, Day 1

No shortcut to perseverance

Up and up they climbed. The trail was relentless with untold numbers of sweeping switchbacks cut into the mountainside. The switchbacks made the trail more manageable in terms of steepness but added considerable length to the route. Occasionally, one of the runners shot straight uphill to intersect the trail above rather than taking the longer route of the switchback. Almost on cue, the others quipped, "Hey, there's no shortcut to fitness." It was a standing joke but it communicated an important message: there's no shortcut to perseverance.

The word *perseverance* has a negative side. Without exception, some level of pain and suffering accompanies it. Otherwise, it wouldn't be perseverance. Though the word is found exclusively in the New Testament, the writer of James refers to Job's perseverance in the Old Testament. Remember that Job was the guy who was stripped of his family, wealth, and health. It almost seems unfair that God used him as an object lesson. Yet Job never, ever lost faith in his God. "You have heard of Job's perseverance and have seen what the Lord finally brought about. The Lord is full of compassion and mercy" (James 5:11b). Job's perseverance through tremendous difficulty—and the Lord's mercy—ultimately brought about good in his life. That's the principle we must embrace.

Every athlete will, sooner or later, have to persevere—hang on for dear life, stay the course, grin and bear it. Eventually, the perseverance pays off, leading to increased fitness and improved performance, along with relief, joy, and gratitude. But it's all too easy to quit on the perilous road to perseverance.

We may not suffer like Job did and lose our family or homes. But an athlete's struggle can become profound, occupying every thought day and night. Repeated injuries and rehab may be the culprit. An inability to nail a tumbling routine can lead to many hard landings and mounting frustration. Going 0 for 4 at the plate—five games in a row—can discourage even a strong-minded player. Sometimes just showing up for another day of practice can break our will. But we must not quit. We must continue.

Easier said than done, huh? How do we continue when our bodies and minds are pleading for us to stop? If the examples of the early saints are any indication (think back to last week's stories of first century suffering), the key seems to be maintaining focus on the end goal. Sure, those goals could be concrete goals such as winning a state title or posting a record time. But if we truly believe God made us the way He did for an express purpose, then our ultimate goal must be to reflect His character in every situation—including athletics.

Team Truth: *As you know, we count as blessed those who have persevered.* (James 5:11a)

Team Time: Do you think it's possible to optimize athletic skill without an element of perseverance? Why or why not? Give an example to support your answer.

____

____

____

____

____

____

____

____

____

____

____

Week 6: Persevering Persistence, Day 2

Tell me again. Why am I doing this?

In the summer of 2011, Jennifer Pharr Davis stood atop Mt. Katahdin at the northern terminus of the Appalachian Trail. Southward she marched, traversing the rocky, rugged peaks and deep valleys. She was on a mission. She had purpose. Everything had been planned out, and she dared not waste one step or an ounce of energy. To complete her self-assigned task, she could not falter even for a day or her dream might collapse. Hike. Hike. Hike. She overcame excruciating pain and overwhelming obstacles. Her world suddenly became very small, her steps pre-determined and her mind focused.

For forty-six days, eleven hours, and twenty minutes, Jen started hiking before the sun rose and continued well after it slipped below the horizon. She sobbed uncontrollably when the shin pain made her legs collapse. She winced every time she shoved swollen and blistered feet back into her shoes. She gagged when she forced much needed calories into her mouth. She relentlessly persevered en route to setting the world speed record on the trail that runs between Maine and Springer

Mountain, Georgia.

But why? Why suffer so much? Why tolerate all the pain? The short answer is that Jennifer had placed her hope in the abilities God gave her and she kept her mind wholly focused.

Paul, a first century apostle, wrote to young Timothy. Imagine how exciting it must have been to receive a letter from the acclaimed missionary. Paul, who regarded Timothy as both a son and a partner in faith, reminded him, "We labor and strive, because we have put our hope in the living God" (1 Timothy 4:10a).

But that's not all. Paul instructed Timothy, "Until I come, devote yourself . . . do not neglect your gift"—in his case, preaching and teaching (1 Timothy 4:13-14). That sure sounds like Paul was telling the young preacher to continue, to persevere.

Why was that so important? You've heard the phrase, "actions speak louder than words." The difference between a person who says they are dedicated and a person who actually demonstrates their dedication is obvious. Steady action becomes a testimony to those watching. That's why Paul stated, "Be diligent in these matters; give yourself wholly to them, so that everyone may see your progress" (1 Timothy 4:15).

Christian athletes have a unique opportunity to practice perseverance. In fact, faith and hope enable them to persevere because they understand that endurance is part of "not neglecting the gift." It's a character trait principled in Scripture and one that speaks volumes in testimony.

Team Truth: *Watch your life and doctrine closely. Persevere in them, because if you do, you will save both yourself and your hearers.* (1 Timothy 4:16)

Team Time: "Be diligent . . . give yourself wholly . . . so that everyone may see your progress" (1 Timothy 4:15). How might this apply to a Christian athlete in terms of both spiritual and athletic perseverance? What consequences result from a lack of diligence?

____

____

____

____

____

____

____

____

Week 6: Persevering Persistence, Day 3

Drop the dead weight

"You've got to be kidding, right?" William asked. The rest of his teammates stared at their coach, eyes wide and lips slightly parted. He couldn't be serious, could he?

"All right. This is the plan. We have a tough practice today. We're going to do a lot of suicides for conditioning. Then, we'll work on rapid-fire lay-ups and jump shots." Though the athletes didn't love the thought of suicides or shooting drills, the next instruction dropped their jaws. "Now, go ahead and get your backpacks and put them on. You'll be wearing them until I tell you to take them off."

Why would a coach do such a thing? Was he mad because his dog bit him? Or maybe he was a former drill instructor looking for a way to take it out on the troops.

The athletes knew better than to argue. Each one picked up his heavy backpack and strapped it on. The first couple of suicides were bad, the next few even worse. Then they began the shooting drills. The backpacks, stuffed with bulky books, clunked against their spines. The boys couldn't jump high or move quickly. Sweat poured off their foreheads, the salt stinging their eyes. This was much harder than they'd anticipated.

Finally, the coach called them to center court. "Okay, fellas. Lose the backpacks. But we're going to do this again." The heavy loads dropped to the floor with resounding thuds. The boys welcomed the drills this time—they'd never felt so light and free. What used to seem like punishment before the backpack escapade now seemed easy. Their perspective was forever changed.

But those athletes weren't the first to make that discovery. The writer of Hebrews knew something about the topic, for he said, "Let us throw off everything that hinders and the sin that so easily entangles. And let us run with perseverance the race marked out for us" (Hebrews 12:1). Of course, he probably wasn't talking specifically about a 5K or marathon runner. But he realized his readers could relate to the analogy. Carrying extra weight is difficult. It slows progress. It's just, well, plain stupid.

Another question remains, however. Once we throw off those things that weigh us down—perhaps stress, conflict, sin, bad relationships, overcrowded schedules, for example—what should we do? We lock our eyes on Jesus and His example of perseverance. It all comes back to focus.

Team Truth: *Let us throw everything that hinders and the sin that so easily entangles. And let us run with perseverance the race marked out for us, fixing our eyes on Jesus, the pioneer and perfecter of faith . . . Consider him who endured . . . so that you will not grow weary and lose heart.* (Hebrews 12:1b-3)

Team Time: What kind of "extra weight" might a team or individual carry that can hinder testimony and/or performance?

____

____

____

____

____

____

____

____

Week 6: Persevering Persistence, Day 4

Good days. Bad days.

It was cold. Very cold. To make matters worse, the winds were strong enough to blow the slight runner into the next county. Nothing was appealing about this workout, but she needed miles.

As she turned west, the full force of the gale slammed into her. Her steps slowed and took on a dream-like quality. No, make that a nightmare. You know the kind. You try to run, to escape, to get away. Your arms pump and legs flail, but sadly, you go nowhere fast. In fact, it all seems slow-mo. That's the way the runner felt. Any desire to continue the fight against the ferocious wind blew down the road.

She was frustrated. Instead of feeling fit and fabulous, she slogged along, hating every step. Her breathing was labored, her legs felt like waterlogged stumps, and worst of all, she felt nothing like an athlete.

When her route finally made a ninety-degree turn, the wind was less severe. With every ounce of energy left, she interjected all-out running efforts. But her "all-out" was still turtle-like. By the time she got home, she was depressed. "Why do I even try?" she moaned.

The sun came up again the next morning. Fancy that. With a couple of other runners, she headed out to mark a race course. When they dropped her off at the trailhead, she watched the car pull away before she stepped onto the wooded trail. She took off, yellow streamers in hand. It was cold again, in the twenties. But this time the air was still. Soon, she was calculating where to hang the next streamer. She ran swiftly—if you discount that she had to stop every seventy-five yards to mark the way. She absorbed the morning crispness, the scampering deer and squirrels, the stillness of the lake's water. She felt like a runner—fast, strong, and powerful—feelings far removed from the previous day's despair.

It's natural to occasionally end a training session or a practice in a slump. We struggle to connect with the ball, score goals, or make shots that should've been easy. But if we want to persevere, we must remember that nothing stays the same. Perseverance produces maturity that cannot be learned in any other way. Perseverance is purposeful, patient plodding that develops character and completeness.

A bad spot, a bad day, even a bad week or month, does not seal the coffin. Hold on to hope. Be encouraged and keep plugging along. Sure, you'll experience good days and bad ones. But even a bad day is good if it means you aren't in the coffin.

Team Truth: *Let perseverance finish its work so that you may be mature and complete, not lacking anything.* (James 1:4)

Team Time: Have you ever been in a slump? Is a teammate struggling? What can you do as an individual and as a team to break free of a slump? What kind of support can you offer?

Week 6: Persevering Persistence, Day 5

Perseverance is part of the plan

Jeff walked onto the court and looked around, excited to join the other guys at the net. Draped across his shoulder was a fancy case that held five expensive racquets, along with balls, extra grips, a towel, and a few energy bars he'd thrown in at the last minute. Brand new court shoes cushioned Jeff's feet, and a sweatband wrapped his wrist. He was ready to become the next tennis phenomenon.

Then the coach walked up. "Okay, guys. Time to get to work." Jeff yanked on the bag's hefty zipper and pulled out a racquet. "Nope. You won't be needing that for a while," said Coach Hill.

"What? This is the tennis team, isn't it? I think we probably need our racquets." Jeff continued to take the racquet from the case. Coach Hill wasn't impressed.

"Jeff. It is Jeff, right?" Jeff nodded. Coach continued. "If you're going to be on my team, you'll have to learn we do things in order. A brilliant tennis player gets that way by building on the basics one step at a time. The sooner you realize that, the better. Now," he said, addressing the entire group, "Let's start off with some conditioning and footwork. Then we'll work on basic ground strokes with the proper grip. That'll be our starting point. Later, we'll add serving, overheads, and volleying. But first things first."

Jeff sheepishly lowered his equipment. He'd learned an important lesson.

Whatever the sport, we probably realize that getting good means climbing the skill ladder one step at a time. We don't go from zero to great without laying a foundation of well-executed basics. And that's not just true about our development as an athlete. Our development as a mature Christian also requires a disciplined, ordered approach.

We tend to think that the ultimate Christian characteristic, love, can be achieved in one step. Not so. For illustrative purposes, assume love is the highest rung on a ladder. To climb that high, we must step on each of the following rungs: faith, goodness, knowledge, self-control, perseverance, godliness, mutual affection, and then love. (See 2 Peter 1:5-7.) No shortcuts. We can't ignore any rung. Each one is equally important—and necessary—if we are to live and love fully.

Isn't it interesting that perseverance is sandwiched between our faith and our ability to love? Until we learn to persevere, we can climb no higher, achieve nothing more. Perseverance in any arena, athletic or otherwise, is absolutely necessary. Embrace it.

Team Truth: *For this very reason, make every effort to add to your faith goodness; and to goodness, knowledge; and to knowledge, self-control; and to self-control, perseverance; and to perseverance, godliness; and to godliness, mutual affection; and to mutual affection, love.* (2 Peter 1:5-7)

Team Time: Fill in the following chart with examples of how each characteristic can be demonstrated in your life and on your team.

	Everyday living	Application to our team/athlete
Faith		
Goodness		
Knowledge		
Self-control		
Perseverance		
Godliness		
Mutual affection		
Love		

Week 7: Falters and Failures, Day 1

L-O-S-E-R

In the height of the 2011-2012 NBA season, Jeremy Lin became a household name. So fanatical were the fans, the phenomenon was dubbed "Linsanity." Madison Square Garden, home of the New York Knicks, turned into a boiling pot whenever Lin hit the hardwood. His picture turned up on the covers of *Time* and *Sports Illustrated*. His jersey was the best-selling NBA clothing item in February 2012. The six foot three inch 200 pounder—small for the NBA—seemed to have it all. But had it always been that way?

Lin, a California native, born to Taiwanese parents, led his high school team to a Division II state championship in 2006. Still, he received no scholarship offers from his colleges of choice: several Ivy League schools, University of California, Berkeley, along with Stanford and UCLA. Only Harvard and Brown promised him spots on their teams, but they offered him no scholarships. (Ivy League schools don't provide athletic scholarships.) Nevertheless, he accepted Harvard's offer despite the fact that one of the assistant coaches considered

Lin nothing more than a Division III-type player.

He left Harvard with a degree in economics and stellar basketball statistics. But when the NBA draft rolled around, no one picked Lin. No one thought he was good enough. However, he participated in an NBA summer training camp and was eventually offered several contracts. He chose to play for his hometown favorite, the Golden State Warriors.

But his contract was not guaranteed, and three times he was relegated to a "developmental" team. Each time, he worked his way back. Then came a serious injury. He spent hours in rehab, increasing his jumping ability and honing the finer points of his game. It all paid off, right? Wrong.

The Warriors dumped Lin to free up money for someone they wanted more. The Houston Rockets picked him up for a total of two preseason games before giving him the boot as well. They, too, wanted to spend their money on another player. After that, the Knicks hired him as the backup to their backup point guard. Word on the street was they, too, were considering ditching Lin. You think Lin felt like a failure?

Then, out of desperation, the coach gave Lin a chance. The team was playing so poorly the coach figured it couldn't get any worse. That was all Lin needed. Since then, the hoopster has been on fire. His response to all this?

"Where is my identity? Is it in being an NBA player or is it in Christ? . . . I have to remember my calling and my purpose on earth is to glorify God in what I do. And right now that is to play basketball . . . I have to play for an audience of one, for God . . . That was liberating for me to be able to lift that burden off of me . . . for me to remember why I am playing . . .”*

Team Truth: *“I have been crucified with Christ and I no longer live, but Christ lives in me.”* (Galatians 2:20a)

Team Time: How does our identity in Christ help us deal with failures and disappointments?

* <http://www.youtube.com/watch?v=J0qrTXZFksQ&feature=share>

Week 7: Falters and Failures, Day 2

Failure follows loss of hope

Rebekah was happy in her Miata convertible, heading west. She planned to rendezvous with her brother John and together run the Mohican 100, a race through the rolling hills of central Ohio. She was excited, confident in her ability to complete the 102-mile distance. She'd run the race previously in under twenty-four hours, and her brother was counting on her to help him achieve his first century finish.

She arrived first at the campground—the headquarters for the start and finish of the race. While she was setting up the tent, her cell phone rang. Her husband delivered devastating news about their oldest son. Their conversation was interrupted by an incoming call. "I have to take this," he said in a despondent voice. A sickening feeling crept into her stomach. When her husband came back on the line, he gave her bad news about their younger son. Rebekah went numb.

Within those few moments, the race lost its appeal and she lost all hope. She felt so lonely, so isolated, so helpless as she sat on a rustic picnic table. "Lord," she cried, "What are you trying to do?" Nausea swept through her. Tears of sorrow ran down her cheeks.

Later, her brother tried to console her, but she couldn't calm down enough to sleep that night. In the morning, they took to the start line. Someone said, "Go," so off they went. Though Rebekah and her brother chatted as they ran through the early morning darkness, she struggled to stay focused. Her body revolted: her urine was scant and brown (a sign of dehydration), she puked constantly when the sun rose higher in the sky, and every muscle cramped due to electrolyte imbalances. Death would've been a relief.

The miles seemed so long. Her tank was empty. Back at the start/finish, which was also mile sixty-five, she thought only about stopping. Running another thirty-seven miles seemed impossible. Why suffer more? She no longer had purpose or hope. Sadly, Rebekah watched her brother run back into the night alone.

You have to be totally engaged in a race like the Mohican 100. It requires a 100 percent commitment: mind, body, and soul. Rebekah didn't have it that day. The stress of knowing her sons' situations weighed on her too heavily. She couldn't work through the pain and the struggle because her heart was not in it. Without unwavering commitment to the task and the hope of completion, the experienced ultrarunner failed miserably.

Hold onto hope. Without it, we won't get very far.

Team Truth: *As for me, I will always have hope; I will praise you more and more.* (Psalm 71:14)

Team Time: Where does hope originate? Can you generate hope yourself? How can you offer hope to others without sounding trite?

____

____

____

____

____

____

____

____

____

____

____

____

Week 7: Falters and Failures, Day 3

Failure (and success) redefined

As athletes we choose to push ourselves even when it's scary, intimidating or painful. But we also must realize that if we attempt to do that in our own power we'll probably fail. Though God fully equips us for appointed tasks, few athletes *really* know what that means. Few experience the rare moment when the impossible becomes possible.

Trey Fisher took to the start line of the 3200-meter state finals. He'd set his heart on breaking the magic ten-minute mark, which he'd narrowly missed by three short seconds in prior races. The gun sounded. Trey stayed toward the back as he settled into the quick pace. After half the distance, he was a full three seconds faster than his race goal. The talented runner worked his way into fourth place in the eighth and final lap, quickly gaining on the third place runner. The pace was furious and intense. Every muscle, every cell in his body was fully engaged, his focus piercing.

A battle ensued down the homestretch. Shoulder to shoulder, Trey contested the race with the third place runner.

Trey pulled ahead, closing in on the finish line. But then everything went black for him. Trey's body betrayed him. Down he went, hard. The crowd gasped. Trey attempted to stand but couldn't. Just ten yards from the finish, he flailed on the track as the runner behind him passed by. Somehow, someway, he crawled across the line before collapsing in a molten heap. The time was 10:03. The crowd, watching in suspense, hushed.

Trey's chest heaved as he tried desperately to catch his breath. His face was white, lips blue. He writhed on the ground in agony, his eyes wild and scared. "I was so close. So close," he whispered.

"Try to slow your breathing," his coach softly advised. Trey looked at her, his eyes communicating deeply as he followed her instructions. They understood each other perfectly. He had run deep and long, traveling to that place where few dare venture.

Getting Trey to sit upright was difficult. Gone were his muscle glycogen stores and his energy reserves. Slowly, a pale, pinkish color replaced the blue tinge around his lips. He looked drained, completely empty. The crowd rose in thunderous ovation when the runner finally stood erect.

Trey was a warrior: a warrior who'd entered the battle prepared to risk failure. He determined to reach deep inside and explore the depths of his soul, the depth of his commitment. He chose to ignore the pain, the agony of oxygen-depleted muscles and heaving lungs, to go beyond, into the abyss.

Trey ran a perfect race—including the ending. He did not fail. His honor, dignity, and courage confirmed his strength of will. Trey boldly credits God who enabled him to venture into the darkness and return to the light.

Team Truth: *My flesh and my heart may fail, but God is the strength of my heart and my portion forever.* (Psalm 73:26)

Team Time: Describe a time when an apparent "failure" was actually a victory.

Week 7: Falters and Failures, Day 4

No "I" in weakness

"Again! When are you going to do it right? You know what to do. Do it now!"

Lindsey choked back the tears. Her teammates had all left the gym, leaving her and Coach alone in the cavernous room. With the district meet coming up the next weekend, the gymnast had to nail this balance beam routine. But she could not master the front aerial walkover—a blind move that could result in catastrophic injury should she miss. Lindsey had watched all the training videos, practiced the move with the aid of the spotting belt hanging from the ceiling, and rehearsed it repeatedly in her head. She knew what to do, but each time she reached that part of her routine, she choked. She felt like a loser, a failure. Little girls half her age successfully threw that trick.

"What's wrong with me?" she finally blubbered. She hated crying in front of her coach and despised the need to ask the question even more. Admitting failure to Coach was hard. She was a big woman with even bigger demands on her athletes.

Lindsey expected a tough rebuke. Instead, Coach motioned her over. "Look, I know you're frustrated, but you're certainly not the first athlete in this position. We all have our weaknesses. But it's those same weaknesses that can make us strong."

Coach continued. "Remember Paul, the first century apostle? He had some kind of ailment that made him feel weak and unsuccessful. He begged God to remove it. But God chose not to heal him. You know why? He didn't want Paul to be conceited in his own power. When Paul accepted his weakness, God was able to demonstrate His power. Now, I'm not saying Paul had to flip around on a balance beam, but there's a lesson in the story. God has given you the knowledge and ability to be a gymnast. He understands your fear. Admit your weakness and rely on God's strength. He's with you on that balance beam just as much as He's present when you're sitting in a worship service. Let Him be your strength."

With that, Lindsey mounted the beam and repeatedly practiced that tough trick. She didn't stick each one but every attempt struck a reminder: weakness does not necessarily result in failure. But failure is certain if we refuse to relinquish our weaknesses.

Team Truth: *Three times I pleaded with the Lord to take it away from me. But he said to me, "My grace is sufficient for you, for my power is made perfect in weakness." Therefore I will boast all the more gladly about my weaknesses, so that Christ's power may* *rest on me. That is why, for Christ's sake, I delight in weaknesses, in insults, in hardships, in persecutions, in difficulties. For when I am weak, then I am strong.* (2 Corinthians 12:8-10)

Team Time: Paul was afflicted with a physical weakness to keep him from being self-reliant. Describe a time when your weakness made you realize you had to rely on Christ's power.

____

____

____

____

____

____

____

____

Week 7: Falters and Failures, Day 5

Life after failure

In the winter of 1998, the Calgary Olympic Games were in full swing. Crouched high above the crowd, Michael Edwards, the sole jumper wearing a Great Britain uniform, prepared to take the 90-meter ski jump. "Eddie the Eagle," as he would later be known, jumped in boots many sizes too big, had horrible form, weighed far too much, and often jumped "blind" when his thick eyeglasses fogged up mid-flight. He took last place in both the 70-meter and the 90-meter hill contests. And yet his "failure" endeared him to the masses. He became an overnight inspiration.

On January 22, 2012, the Baltimore Ravens battled the New England Patriots in a divisional playoff game. Eleven seconds remained on the clock. Baltimore was down by three. Billy Cundiff stepped onto the field to attempt a 32-yard field goal, a kick he'd made hundreds of times. The crowd hushed as they watched the ball's flight path. Then, in an instantaneous roar, the home crowd erupted when Billy's kick failed to direct the ball between the uprights. There'd be no overtime. New

England moved forward. Baltimore went home.

These examples represent two kinds of failures. In Edward's case, no one expected much, so it was more of a personal conquest than an out-and-out failure. But Cundiff's story is different. Everyone had huge expectations. As an experienced NFL kicker, he could make a 32-yarder in his sleep. He hadn't missed a fourth quarter kick in over two years. Only that time, he did miss. His failure was more than personal. It ended his team's bid for the AFC championship and the opportunity to play in the Super Bowl.

How do we react to falters and failures? Does the world come to an end? Do we quit? Consider this. Long ago, a descendant of the famous King David, Abijah, became king of Judah. Not because he was a good man. The ancient writer tells us that Abijah's heart was not devoted to God and that he habitually committed the same sins as his father, Rehoboam. "Nevertheless, for David's sake" God made Jerusalem strong during Abijah's reign (1 Kings 15:4).

For David's sake? But why? Was David perfect? Nope. "For David had done what was right in the eyes of the LORD and had not failed to keep any of the LORD's commands all the days of his life—except in the case of Uriah the Hittite" (1 Kings 15:5). Oops! That Uriah incident involved adultery and murder, a bit more of a failure than missing a field goal. And yet God was gracious. David's failure was forgiven because he repented.

No doubt, failures are tough to handle. But those inevitable failures should cause us to refocus on the big picture. Failures should mature us, inspire growth, and impart valuable lessons. Be encouraged. Failure is not fatal.

Team Truth: *But you, Lord, are a compassionate and gracious God, slow to anger, abounding in love and faithfulness.* (Psalm 86:15)

Team Time: Based on Psalm 86:15, what should be our principled response when a teammate fails? Give a real-life example of when/how this concept could be applied.

Week 8: Service with a Smile, Day 1

Want fries with that?

Think about the last time you walked into a fast-food restaurant. How were you greeted? Did you feel as if you were a welcomed guest or an annoying distraction to a conversation going on behind the counter? If it was the latter, maybe more than the food itself left a bad taste in your mouth.

So what does ordering a burger and fries have to do with athletics? That's a fair question. We normally don't think of sports as being an opportunity to serve, but if we aren't careful, our bad service—or lack of service—can leave a bad taste in someone's mouth. And if we truly believe that our athletic abilities have been given to us for the express purpose of bringing God glory, then we must consider how we can use those talents to glorify God through service.

We typically think of the word *serve* in the context of "servant." It carries the connotation of being an underling—someone obligated to tend to the needs of another. Not many of us welcome that idea. Who wants to be at the beck and call of someone else? It's unnatural to lay aside personal desires for someone else's benefit.

The first thing we have to decide is this: Whom are we to serve? From a biblical perspective, there are two good choices. First, we are to "fear the LORD your God, [and] serve him only" (Deuteronomy 6:13). But we're also to "serve others" and not ourselves (1 Peter 4:10). In both cases, service is an outward expression of an inward mindset. So, let's start looking at this mindset of service to God since it's the foundation for service to others.

Another word for mindset is attitude. We probably all know someone who has "served" in some way but for all the wrong reasons. Maybe they wanted credit for being a great guy or for giving a lot of time or money. However, serving with the wrong motive is actually a lie.

It's important, therefore, to understand what our attitude should be when we serve both God and other people. Once we lay that foundation, we'll be able to apply those principles to real-life situations throughout the coming week.

Team Truth: *But be very careful to keep the commandment and the law that Moses the servant of the LORD gave you: to love the LORD your God, to walk in obedience to him, to keep his commands, to hold fast to him and to serve him with all your heart and with all your soul.* (Joshua 22:5)

Team Time: Look up the following verses and complete the chart. The first one is done as an example.

Reference	How to serve
*Deuteronomy 10:12	Wholeheartedly
Joshua 24:14	
1 Chronicles 23:31	
Psalm 130:4	
Acts 20:19	
Galatians 5:13	
1 Peter 4:11	
1 Peter 5:2	

*Use the 2011 edition of the NIV for best results.

Week 8: Service with a Smile, Day 2

Cut to the core

"Tebowing" refers to the one-knee praying position of NFL quarterback Tim Tebow. He worked his way into the public arena by ferocious, effective play despite the lack of perfect technique. But his unconventional throwing style didn't stop him from leading his team to unbelievable comeback victories. Those wins, along with bowed head and bent knee, showed the world whom he represented.

And who was that? In every interview, Tebow acknowledged his (then) Denver-based football team. He proudly wore the uniform and spoke highly of the organization. A lot rides on public perception, and Tebow didn't say or do anything that discredited the Mile High City's home team. He understood that if he made a bad play on—or off—the field, the team's reputation would be affected by his actions.

But Tebow also recognizes a higher calling. His longstanding faith has formed and shaped his priorities. He was, and still is, quick to give unashamed testimony to his faith in the Lord Jesus Christ. And his actions speak even louder than his words.

Tebow puts his faith to work in practical ways. He uses uplifting, encouraging language with both his teammates and his competitors. Always respectful, he's mindful of what comes out of his mouth, knowing that one ugly outburst could destroy his testimony. But being a "good dooby" is only the beginning.

Even before graduating from college, Tebow established the "First and 15" organization with the blessing of the NCAA and the University of Florida. He coordinated volunteerism and fundraising on behalf of Philippine orphanages and sick kids in his community. Once he entered the NFL, he put his fame and accompanying wealth to good use by establishing the Tim Tebow Foundation. A number of programs have been established to serve specific needs of sick children, hospital facilities, and the underprivileged.

Why? Tebow's core values come from Philippians 4:8-9. He's connected the dots between belief and action. Therefore, if anything is truthful, noble, just, pure, lovely, of good report, virtuous, and highly praised, Tim Tebow steps off the field and into the streets in order to serve his fellow man.

Team Truth: *Finally, brothers and sisters, whatever is true, whatever is noble, whatever is right, whatever is pure, whatever is lovely, whatever is admirable—if anything is excellent or praiseworthy—think about such things. Whatever you have learned* *or received or heard from me, or seen in me—put it into practice. And the God of peace will be with you.* (Philippians 4:8-9)

Team Time: What are your core values, personally or as a team? What kind of service projects could come out of those beliefs?

____

____

____

____

____

____

____

____

____

Week 8: Service with a Smile, Day 3

Serve as if . . .

Have you ever thought of your team as a business? It might seem weird, but if we understand the similarities, we can identify our customers, provide outstanding service, and extend our outreach.

Let's start by defining various roles. In a school team setting, the board of directors is probably the school board. They, in turn, appoint the athletic director as president and CEO of the athletic division. Where does that put the coach? He might be a senior vice-president with the assistant coaches serving as his administrative assistants. The team captain is a supervisor and each team member is an employee, some (seniors) with more benefits than others (freshmen).

Now that we've defined a team in a business context, we should think about our customers. Remember, a customer is anyone who has a need we can fill. As a division of the corporation, the team is obligated to satisfy the needs of the leadership. That might be in terms of numbers and records, excellence, and establishing a goal for the team. If the owners aren't happy, nobody's happy.

But what about external customers? Parents, friends, and sports fans have a vested interest in the team. They provide the time and resources that assure the team's success. The athletes' younger brothers and sisters are also customers in that they look to the team for role modeling, whether they understand that or not. And paying customers dole out hard-earned money at the gate in order to watch the team play.

How can we possibly make all those people happy? Let's look at a parallel example from the first century. The apostle Paul wrote to the church at Ephesus from a prison cell. In his letter he gave them instructions about their role in society. Some of the Ephesians wondered why they should still be slaves to their masters. Hadn't Christ free them from all that? Nope. Think again.

Paul gave one overriding principle that indicated how those Christians should approach their role in the "slave" company. He says, "Serve wholeheartedly, as if you were serving the Lord, not people" (Ephesians 6:7). It doesn't matter if you like them or not.

A successful team will understand that the highest customer satisfaction marks come from adopting a similar attitude: Whatever our circumstances may be, we serve an audience of one, Jesus Christ. Serve with all your heart, all the time.

Team Truth: *Obey them not only to win their favor when their eye is on you, but as slaves of Christ, doing the will of God from your heart. Serve wholeheartedly, as if you were serving the Lord, not people, because you know that the Lord will reward each one for whatever good they do, whether they are slave or free.* (Ephesians 6:6-8)

Team Time: You've probably heard the phrase, "doing it for all the wrong reasons." How might the principle found in Ephesians 6 prevent you from serving with wrong motives?

Week 8: Service with a Smile, Day 4

Using whatever

It began as a fleeting thought. But when it returned over and over again, the coach could ignore it no longer.

She'd randomly noticed a Facebook discussion about a mission trip to Costa Rica. *What if* . . . she mused. *What if we could get a group of athletes together? We could use our talents as a platform to reach others.* Her excitement grew as wildly as Jack's beanstalk when she considered the possibilities. A few phone calls later, she was standing in front of her team sharing the vision.

The trip was under the auspices of Hands of Compassion International, based in Appomattox, Virginia. Though this group had been coordinating short-term mission efforts for several years, they hadn't been involved in sports-related trips. Still, connections with the missionaries in Costa Rica and their contacts with SCORE International, a Christian athletic mission organization, set the wheels turning.

Before they knew it, a dozen female athletes from Liberty Christian Academy, along with their coach and leaders, boarded a plane for Costa Rica. For some, it was a first-ever experience to take off into the friendly skies. They were headed to a foreign country equipped to perform mime skits with a message, play lots of soccer, teach volleyball skills, and share their faith.

The ten-day trip was filled with work in schools and communities. The hours were exhausting; the opportunities were many. Each team member returned with a much greater appreciation for how they could effectively use their God-given gifts.

It's actually similar in concept to the early church described in 1 Peter. The writer gives a reminder, paraphrased like this: "Okay. Time to get real. You guys should be done with sin. No more drunkenness. No more debauchery. No more lust. No more reckless, wild living. You have better things to do" (1 Peter 4:1-6).

And what were the readers supposed to do to replace their wicked ways? First, clear their minds so they could pray. Then, they were to love deeply and be happily hospitable. And the next step? Listen up. "Each of you use whatever gift you have received to serve others, as faithful stewards of God's grace in its various forms" (1 Peter 4:10).

God gives each of us different gifts for different reasons. It's our responsibility to make a conscious decision to put those gifts to good use. And we can be confident that God will give us the strength and support we need to serve effectively.

Team Truth: *If anyone serves, they should do so with the strength God provides, so that in all things God may be praised through Jesus Christ. To him be the glory and the power for ever and ever. Amen.* (1 Peter 4:11b)

Team Time: It may not be possible for every team to travel to a foreign country. (But it may be more feasible than you think.) Use this time to brainstorm ideas for service projects in your community or in another country.

____

____

____

____

____

____

____

____

Week 8: Service with a Smile, Day 5

Hands-on service

We've been discussing service all week. We've established a biblical need for service, how service should be delivered, and whom we should serve. But there haven't been a lot of concrete ideas for athletic teams. Of course, service begins in the heart but the hands must fulfill it. Today, we'll look at four real-life teams and how they choose to serve.

Berry College, Mount Berry, Georgia: Each semester, this NCAA D-III school gathers nearly all its 300 plus athletes. On a designated day, the student athletes disperse to schools, community centers, libraries, homeless shelters, thrift stores, or wherever a need has emerged. There, they eagerly help the organizations accomplish necessary tasks. These work days have been coordinated by the student athlete-run ABC (Athletes Bettering the Community). Additionally, various sports teams have taken on fundraising projects for kids with cancer, support for soldiers, and medical research.

Tennessee Tech, Cookesville, Tennessee: In 2011, student athletes donated over 3,000 hours of volunteer service time.

They participated in Fall Fun Fest, Hoops for Heroes, Habitat for Humanity building projects, coaching Upward Sports at local churches, reading in schools, volunteering at the Mustard Seed Ranch, and many other individual and group service projects. Says athletic director Mark Wilson, "They not only represent the University and athletics in a positive manner, but they also represent themselves as first-class young women and men."*

Doane College, Crete, Nebraska: The track team takes service to their community very seriously. Once a month, each of the thirty members donates a minimum of thirty minutes to the area's elementary schools. Senior captain Edwin Ronoh says, "Good character can be defined as courage, compassion, integrity, fairness, self-control, responsibility, leadership and respect . . . It is important to incorporate all these aspects of character into a team in order to succeed. Each individual becomes part of the process because they hold each other accountable for the high standards. Working together as a team with courage and with passion has led us to many victories, both individually and as a team."** The men's track team was awarded the 2011 NAIA Champions of Character Award.

Jamestown College, Jamestown, North Dakota: This small school of 1,000 students also values service. Each athletic team participates in at least one service project per season. Some of the activities include Hoops for Heart, Elementary Reading Program, food banks, mentoring for kids, and many other projects.

Team Truth: *Whoever serves me must follow me; and where I am, my servant also will be. My Father will honor the one who serves me.* (John 12:26)

Team Time: Get organized. Decide on a team service project and start planning!

____

____

____

____

____

____

____

____

____

*<http://www.ttusports.com/releases/2011-12/1_1__service_hours>

**<http://www.doane.edu/news/champions-of-character/>

Week 9: Go Team, Day 1

Stir it up

The group of young naval officers headed to the track. This was it. A final test of physical fitness. Run the prescribed time and move on. Fall short, go home. Some would complete the task easily. For others, it would prove more difficult than heading to the front lines.

The early morning sky was still dark. But sleepiness wasn't an option. Each officer candidate needed to run the mile and a half in 10:30. The drill instructor gave the command; the young men began their attack on the required six laps. Round and round they went, straining for the finish. One young man, Johnson, crossed the line well under the standard and moved off to the side to watch his comrades. He noticed one of his classmates struggling on the far side of the track. He glanced at the clock and realized his classmate had little chance of making the cutoff. He had to do something—success for the unit meant bringing everyone home in the allotted time.

Johnson took off in the opposite direction. The drill instructor yelled, "Where do you think you're going, Johnson?

Get back here. Listen to me, you $*^%*#(@^!" The vulgarities kept coming but Johnson kept going. He wondered if he had made a career-ending decision.

When he came alongside the lagging soldier, Johnson did all he could to urge him to move faster. "Pick it up! Move! You gotta do this!" All the while, the drill instructor continued his barrage of insults and his demands to return. As the duo rounded the last curve and headed down the homestretch, every eye was fixed on them. The clock clicked ever closer to 10:30. The soldier's chest heaved from the effort to cross the line in time. One last step stopped the incessant ticking. Exactly 10:30. He made it because he was spurred on by someone who cared.

"Johnson. Get over here!"

Uh-oh. Here it comes.

But the drill instructor surprised him: "Johnson. Well done. You understand that whatever the risk, the team is only as good as the weakest man. You understood the mission—get everyone home. You rightly defied my order for the sake of your teammate. You have what it takes to be a naval officer."

Do we have what it takes? God has intentionally placed us together as a team for a purpose: to reflect His glory; to see our team in the bigger picture of God's plan and message; and to encourage, uphold, and challenge each other. But we'll never be able to function well if we don't "hold unswervingly to the hope we profess."

Team Truth: *Let us hold unswervingly to the hope we profess, for he who promised is faithful. And let us consider how we may spur one another on toward love and good deeds.* (Hebrews 10:23-24)

Team Time: Johnson's actions resulted in success for his fellow officer. What kind of emotions or obstacles did Johnson have to overcome in order to help? How can you apply this to other situations?

Week 9: Go Team, Day 2

Team talk-n'

The 2011 New Covenant Schools' soccer team gathered moments prior to the Division II title game at the National Association of Christian Athletes tournament in Dayton, TN. The coach handed his captain a piece of paper. "Josh, would you please read this to the team? Drew [a former player] sent us a message."

The team listened intently, absorbing every word like a thirsty, dry sponge:

> Well, team, it's the big day: Championship Friday. Word has spread that you guys have put on a great show thus far and, judging from the brackets, you certainly have. The NCS soccer team hasn't been in this good of a position since this day six years ago, the same day they took home the title. I have faith that today your team, or should I say, 'our team,' has a legitimate shot at a Division II title . . . No pressure. I'm sure you know you have the backing of your fellow students and faculty, but you also have the backing of your former students and

> teammates. Just remember that for some of you it will be your last shot that many of us former players never had. And for you non-seniors, understand you guys are partaking in something almost sanctified in the eyes of many . . . Enjoy it. Today is a very special day for you. Go out there and play with intensity, leaving it all on the field, knowing that some day you can look back and be proud . . . Finally, play being mindful of who you're playing for, the name of the school on your jersey, and the name of your Savior on your heart . . . Break a leg, Gryphons. Beat Chattanooga. Win or lose, I couldn't be more proud of you guys.

The room fell silent, except for sniffles wiped away on shirtsleeves. The message penetrated, the soothing ointment of words seeping into every rusted cranny of the players' souls. The significance of who they were and whom they represented provided the fuel needed to ignite the spark. They cried together, prayed together, and went out and won together.

Drew's letter reminded the NCS soccer team of their connection to things much bigger than themselves. The 2011 team wasn't an island. It was just one more set of waves that followed all the others to the shore, part of a constant tide that rolled in and out. They, like the team six years prior, simply capitalized on the opportunity to ride a huge swell.

Members of a team must see themselves as part of a bigger picture, or they risk becoming self-absorbed. It's like a believer who understands that he functions with the millions who came before him and those coming after him in the body of Christ. Embracing our heritage—being mindful of who we are and from where we've come—makes all the difference in the world.

Team Truth: *For I have always been mindful of your unfailing love and have lived in reliance on your faithfulness.* (Psalm 26:3)

Team Time: Recount your team's history. What part of *then* impacts your *now*?

____

____

____

____

____

____

____

____

____

Week 9: Go Team, Day 3

Weak and wobbly

In the wee hours of the morning, three soggy, wet women stepped back onto the narrow trail after a not-so-restful, rainy rest. A black bear had invaded the camp and sauntered into their three-sided shelter in search of food. It eventually fled. But now, the runners shared the woods with the bear as they continued the journey. Every snap of a branch or rustle in the forest made them wonder if it was stalking them. Still, they had to claim one more peak, and then another, and many more if they were to accomplish their goal.

They were determined to set a record on the South Beyond 6000: to summit forty North Carolina peaks in excess of 6,000 feet elevation in five separate mountain ranges, covering the nearly 300 mile distance on foot. At least fifteen of those peaks bore no trails leading to their summits. Rather, it took flesh-tearing bushwhacking and orienteering to find the exact spot that would lead them to the top of each peak. The three friends—Rebekah Trittipoe, Anne Lundblad, and Jenny Anderson—sought the women's best mark for this undertaking.

In the darkness of the second morning, they set off to find the next peak. Though the summit was a mere third of a mile off the trail, finding a route to the top was nearly impossible. There was no trail. The wet ground was slippery. And blow-downs blocked the way up a very steep mountainside. The trio struggled for an hour before clawing their way to the top. The traverse down, nearly as difficult as the ascent, gave way to brisk running when feet met trail once again.

But a problem arose. Anne and Jenny sped ahead, worried about making up for lost time. Rebekah, age 52, fell behind, unable to maintain the same pace. Frustrated, she felt her anger rising. The younger women, ages 42 and 34, became equally frustrated at the elder runner's snail-like pace. Something had to give.

On top of the next mountain, amid a flood of tears, Rebekah blurted, "Look. You guys are killing me. If this is the way you want it, fine. I'll quit and let you go on. I told you before, we can only go as fast as the slowest person—and that's me!"

Voices rose higher than the peak on which they stood as the discussion became more emotional. But in the end, the women cried and worked it out. They decided to run in birth order, allowing Rebekah to set the pace. But she had to hold up her end of the deal and keep the train rolling. It worked. Without the pressure to keep up from behind, Rebekah led the way. They followed that plan each day. And after six days, thirteen hours, and thirty-one minutes, the three stood atop the last peak. Success.

A team has little chance to succeed if it ignores its weaknesses. In this case, success required tough words, a plan for progress, and everyone's best effort. Painful? Yes. But necessary.

Team Truth: *As iron sharpens iron, so one person sharpens another.* (Proverbs 27:16)

Team Time: How can teammates hold each other accountable without ruining relationships or bossing people around?

____

____

____

____

____

____

____

____

Week 9: Go Team, Day 4

BFFs

Did you ever pour over the Sears Christmas catalog as a child? Hundreds of pages conjured up visions of what it'd be like to have an Easy Bake Oven or a Creepy Crawler Thingmaker. But besides toys, the catalog also contained sections for home goods and appliances. Even a youngster could see the pattern. The catalog writers promoted their goods as a value continuum: good, better, best. Let's apply that to friendships.

A team is a great place to find *good* friends. You know the type. We remember their nicknames, carry on conversations, and share a few laughs. They're far more than acquaintances, but we won't spill our guts to them. Most of us could fill an entire page with the names of these friends.

Then we have *better* friends. The relationship goes a little deeper. We might get together for activities. The walls of our lives become more transparent and our inadequacies more difficult to hide. But still, a back hallway remains off limits, some things better left untouched. The names of these friends could also fill a page—as long as it isn't the size of a legal pad.

Finally, we have those friends, those teammates, who are extraordinary and *best*. Whether difficulties strike hard or good news comes out of nowhere, you text them first. They ask uncomfortable questions but also know when to shut up. They encourage. They take extra care not to discourage. They laugh and cry with you. When they say they'll pray, they do. When they say they'll help, they come armed. They embrace your best interest. Even when circumstances or miles separate, these friendships cannot be extinguished. We're fortunate if the names of these *best* friends fill a small card. Actually, make that a Post-it Note.

One group of such friends called themselves the "Sisters of Mercy." They held "therapy sessions"—hair colored and toenails painted in the process. No pretense of perfection. Just simple honesty. They established a code of respect about what was said and what should never be repeated. The Sisters were quick to aid the one who hurt. They allowed themselves to act goofy and look ridiculous. They loved, laughed, hugged, encouraged, commiserated, and yes, admonished when necessary—like the characters in *The Sisterhood of the Traveling Pants*, only better. Their bond wasn't based on emotion, or convenience, or similarities. Their appearance was as different as night and day, salt and pepper, hot and cold. What held them together in sisterhood was their Father in heaven.

Work hard to cultivate at least one Post-it Note friend on your team.

Team Truth: *If one falls down, his friend can help him up. But pity the man who falls and has no one to help him up!* (Ecclesiastes 4:10)

Team Time: Having a best buddy (or two) is vital. However, having tightly bound friends can be counterproductive to a sense of "team." What precautions can you take to avoid isolating people? Or isolating the entire team from anyone on the outside?

Week 9: Go Team, Day 5

Game plan

The church in ancient Corinth had everything: the good, the bad, and the ugly. The city was well situated on a four-mile-wide isthmus between the Aegean and Ionian seas. The danger of sailing around the tip of the isthmus made it more prudent to haul entire ships across the land on rollers rather than to risk death at sea. Luckily for Corinth, the ships were dragged right through the middle of the city, making it a popular place. On a nearby mountain an impenetrable fort, Acrocorinth, stood poised to protect the city below.

Historians estimate the population of the city at one million and upwards to six million people. It was the capital of Achaia, a Roman province that included almost all of Greece. But the Greeks didn't fully lay claim to the city. Many Romans moved there along with other nationalities, including Jews, wooed by its great prosperity. The Corinthians worshiped both Greek and Roman gods. Nevertheless, a group of believers established a church in the middle of the chaos when the apostle Paul visited the city for about eighteen months on his second missionary journey.

Once Paul left, the church, made up of both Jews and Gentiles (non-Jews) got a little confused from time to time. They were caught up in immorality, and they had ethical questions about involvement in their culture. As a result, they ended up with many factions. False teachers slipped in unnoticed. Paul wrote them two letters in an attempt to straighten them out. By the time the second letter arrived, the church had returned somewhat to the truth, but the relationship between Paul and the church was strained. A tough situation.

In the end, Paul concludes the second letter by begging them to look deep into their souls. He doesn't want to be harsh with them because the Lord had given him the authority to build them up, not to tear them down.

In the closing verses, he gives this team of Christians a game plan for success. First, make sure you are in the faith, part of God's team. Second, do right, not wrong. Third, rejoice. Be happy! But that's not all. He also asks this group of believers to interact in such a way that promotes and strengthens the team. They were to become fully restored in their faith, encourage each other, have a single-minded purpose, and live in peace (2 Corinthians 13:5-10).

Any team that wants to be successful is wise to do likewise.

Team Truth: *Finally, brothers and sisters, rejoice! Strive for full restoration, encourage one another, be of one mind, live in peace. And the God of love and peace will be with you.* (2 Corinthians 13:11)

Team Time: The way believers (the church) are to interact parallels the way a team should function. Use the chart below to come up with examples of what this might look like on a team. Be specific.

Restoration	
Encouragement	
Single-minded purpose	
Live in peace	

Week 10: In Pursuit of Excellence, Day 1

Practice makes perfect

"Again. Keep shooting."

Toby glared at his coach. He'd been taking this same shot at goal for fifteen minutes—after shooting at least that long from the other side of the field. His legs felt like they might fall off. As the highest scoring striker on the soccer team, he really didn't see the point in rehearsing this skill over and over again. He was already good enough to make the all-conference team and win just about every offensive player award. Enough was enough. This workout, to Toby, was complete overkill.

Then there was Rachel. She wasn't quite the star Toby was, but she was a member of the swim team. Unfortunately, the girl was out of shape, wasn't very skilled in a couple of the strokes, and had little chance of swimming in a varsity meet. Still, she saw the team as a way to spend time with her friends—when it was convenient.

One workout was particularly challenging for Rachel: 400 meters each of back, butterfly, breast, and free. The pace had to be brisk. The team hit the pool, sending the sound of splashing water echoing across the natatorium. Most of the swimmers worked hard. But not Rachel. Her coach watched as Rachel cheated on the number of laps, took long rests, and swam at a pace that barely raised her heart rate off of baseline. When confronted, she simply said, “What’s the big deal? I’m no good anyway. Doing something is better than nothing.”

Was Rachel right? Did Toby have a point? Should both individuals be content with the status quo? Does our attitude about striving for excellence and doing the best we can have anything to do with God’s intentions?

An incident in the Old Testament suggests that God expects our best and equips us to do it. Moses received instructions from God about building the tabernacle and all its related furnishings, including the Ark of the Covenant. Moses wasn’t a craftsman but others were. A guy named Bezalel was filled with God’s spirit, given wisdom, understanding, knowledge, and skills “to make artistic designs for work in gold, silver and bronze, to cut and set stones, to work in wood, and to engage in all kinds of crafts” (Exodus 31:4-5). He was given a teammate, Oholiab, to help him achieve excellence.

Do you think God equipped them with those skills so they could do a half-hearted, it’s-good-enough kind of job? Doubtful. Perhaps God didn’t give us the skills to be craftsmen, but He expects the skills—athletic and otherwise—that He intentionally gave to us to be fully developed and used for His glory.

Team Truth: *Also I have given ability to all the skilled workers to make everything I have commanded you.* (Exodus 31:6b)

Team Time: True or false? "It's the attitude that counts." Explain your answer.

___

___

___

___

___

___

___

___

___

___

___

Week 10: In Pursuit of Excellence, Day 2

If you get it, give it.

Do you remember the stories about Toby and Rachel from yesterday's lesson? Toby was athletically talented. He had speed and quickness, and he consistently put the ball in the net. On the other hand, the information about Rachel, the swimmer, indicated that she wouldn't be qualifying for the Olympics anytime soon. Do both athletes have equal responsibilities when it comes to effort and performance expectations?

Part of the answer is found in an ancient parable. Dr. Luke records a conversation between Jesus and Peter (Luke 12:42-48). The issue concerns who is considered a faithful, wise manager and the story goes like this: The master picks a servant to be in charge of feeding all the other servants while he is away. The good servant is the one who completes his assignments as though the master could come back any minute. In contrast, the bad servant is the one who takes advantage of the fact that the master is away. He beats his charges and makes them go hungry.

Jesus says, "Shame on you if you know what to do and still do wrong. You'll pay for that! If you did wrong without knowing what was expected, you'll still be punished—but not as much" (Luke 12:47, paraphrased).

The punch line? "From everyone who has been given much, much will be demanded; and from the one who has been entrusted with much, much more will be asked" (Luke 12:48b).

Jesus often taught in parables. In this story He emphasized the importance of God's servants being responsible and prepared at all times. Of course, Jesus doesn't address soccer players or swimmers in the passage, but we can apply at least two general principles to athletics (or music, or art, or cooking, or anything else).

First, we're obligated to do exactly as expected even when the master (in this case, the coach) isn't around. Successful athletes don't wait for the coach to tell them what to do, nor do they take a break when the coach looks away. Rather, successful athletes are intrinsically motivated to prepare well regardless of whose eyes may—or may not—be watching. They don't require a taskmaster to beat them into doing their workouts.

"He isn't working up to his potential" is a common description of very talented people who are satisfied with less than their best because their less is still as good as someone less talented. That's unfortunate because the other principle Jesus taught is that we are responsible to fully use what we are given. If we're given a lot of talent, we better use all of it. Anything less makes us an unworthy servant.

Team Truth: *From everyone who has been given much, much will be demanded; and from the one who has been entrusted with much, much more will be asked.* (Luke 12:48b)

Team Time: If everyone on the team truly gives their best, can we expect everyone's *actual* performance level to be the same? Why or why not?

Week 10: In Pursuit of Excellence, Day 3

Heart and soul

The late afternoon sun seemed hotter than normal for an early spring day in the heart of Texas. Everyone was dragging. As the boys shuffled to the practice field, bat bags hanging from their shoulders, their conversation was as listless as the non-existent breeze.

"Can't wait to get home," John said. "I'm so done with school and baseball. Just get me out of here!"

His buddy Matt agreed. "I feel ya. And I sure hope Coach doesn't have us do those fielding drills we hate. That'd be a terrible way to end the week."

The team crowded into the dugout when Coach called them over. "Fellas, we have work to do today. We made some big mistakes in Tuesday's game. Very sloppy play. We have to do better if we're going to beat Chaparral next week. So, this is what we're gonna do . . ."

Matt and John groaned out loud as Coach explained the workout—exactly what they didn't want to do. Coach threw them a sideways glance before walking up the steps and onto the field. "Let's go, guys. Chop. Chop. Give me your best today."

Coach hit countless balls into the outfield for Matt and John to handle. When they continuously refused to run hard in chasing down grounders and exerted minimal effort to catch fly balls they thought were out of reach, Coach called them over. "You're done. If you can't give me heart and soul, you don't need to be on the field." The boys hung their heads as they retreated to the locker room. Message received.

Sound familiar? Of course it's hard to be "up" every day. Is the whole idea of giving heart and soul to our endeavors (sports, school, music, etc.) even valid? It's so much work!

The prophet Jeremiah gives a rather surprising glimpse into the character of God. In chapter 32, the prophet quotes God: "And they shall be my people, and I will be their God: And I will give them one heart, and one way, that they may fear me forever, for the good of them, and of their children after them" (vv. 38-39). But then it gets really interesting.

God is a spirit and this isn't a debate on what form He takes. However, God is committed to His people and says, "I . . . will assuredly plant them in this land with all my heart and soul" (Jeremiah 32:41).

All His heart and soul? If God performs His work with "heart and soul," that's a clear indication of how we should approach our duties, tasks, and responsibilities.

Team Truth: *I will rejoice in doing them good and will assuredly plant them in this land with all my heart and soul.* (Jeremiah 32:41)

Team Time: Does having an "all my heart and soul" attitude mean that athletes should go "full out" all the time? Should you play volleyball at a family picnic like it's the Olympics, slamming the ball into Granny's face? How can you strike a balance and still reflect "heart and soul"? Does it relate to commitment in any way?

Week 10: In Pursuit of Excellence, Day 4

Work like a slave

Imagine that you're living in the first century in southwest Asia Minor. Your hometown is Collosae, a Roman province. Only thing is, you're not Roman. You're a Jewish immigrant working as a slave.

You rise before dawn and head off to the textile mill. A once booming metropolis, the town has fallen into hard times. That spells trouble for you. You have to work harder and longer in order to please your masters. They expect you to work without breaks and barely allow any time for a meal. What's more, they don't seem to care that you have a family and responsibilities at home. Being happy in your situation is nearly impossible.

Then a letter comes from an imprisoned missionary. You never met the guy but you've heard a lot about him. The church you attend gathers together as news of the letter's arrival spreads. What could he possibly say?

You can hardly believe your ears when the elder reads, "Slaves, obey your earthly masters in everything; and do it, not only when their eye is on you and to curry their favor, but with sincerity of heart and reverence for the Lord" (Colossian 3:22).

"WHAT? You gotta be joking me! That doesn't seem right."

Now, let's say you feel somewhat like that slave. Your coach demands your time and he insists that you do things his way, teachers pile on work, and your parents expect you to help at home. You feel like everyone, except you, controls your life. And you don't like it one little bit.

The principle found in this letter to the Colossians is relevant to our topic of excellence. The slaves weren't supposed to do half-hearted work. They weren't to quit working when the boss wasn't looking. Paul asked them to honor God by obeying their masters and by giving them exceptional service. Furthermore, they weren't to do it to win brownie points. Nope. They were to do so because God expected them to do it.

Can you see why an athlete is required to do his best at all times? Whether or not we feel like slaves, we're expected to work like God is our master: we're to be happy and content, striving for excellence because that's the testimony He desires.

Team Truth: *Whatever you do, work at it with all your heart, as working for the Lord, not for human masters, since you know that you will receive an inheritance from the Lord as a reward.* (Colossians 3:23)

Team Time: Do you know someone who's an example of this principle? Specifically, what do they do or say that demonstrates their desire for excellence?

____

____

____

____

____

____

____

____

Week 10: In Pursuit of Excellence, Day 5

Why be good?

Micah Brickhill, a high school senior, is more than any parent, coach, or teacher could ask for. This girl does it all. She excels academically, earning high grades and scoring in the top percentiles of the college entrance exam, the SAT. On the track, she flies around the oval to win races, records falling in her rocket-like wake. Her diligence and hard work, in season and out, are impossible to miss. Micah is coachable and eager to learn. She is the quintessential scholar-athlete.

But that's not all. Micah conducts herself in such a way that people are drawn to her. It's not that she desires rock star attention. Rather, with a quiet and kind aura she embraces people, interacting with them sincerely. She looks for ways to serve. Micah gives without thought of getting, works when no one else will, and loves with both her heart and hands.

Was Micah born perfect? Of course not. But Micah obviously understands the principles written in the book of Titus.

The writer reminds Titus of how Christians are expected to

live: be obedient to authority, look for ways to do good at all times, watch what you say about other people, be considerate and peaceable, and always be gentle with everyone.

Those tall orders don't come naturally. It's much easier to be disobedient, selfish, controlled by anger, and swayed by inappropriate passions. But something happens when we're changed from the inside out. Consider this:

"But when the kindness and love of God our Savior appeared, he saved us, not because of righteous things we had done, but because of his mercy. He saved us through the washing of rebirth and renewal by the Holy Spirit, whom he poured out on us generously through Jesus Christ our Savior, so that, having been justified by his grace, we might become heirs having the hope of eternal life." (Titus 3:4-7)

Micah has been renewed by love for her Savior. Her life plays out differently because she *is* a different person. She has freedom to pursue excellence in all her endeavors: personal relationships, school, sports, family, and service. She can—and does—devote herself to doing what is good.

Team Truth: *This is a trustworthy saying. And I want you to stress these things, so that those who have trusted in God may be careful to devote themselves to doing what is good. These things are excellent and profitable for everyone.* (Titus 3:8)

Team Time: Doing good is considered useful and excellent. What are some specific ways you can pursue excellence (doing good) through actions?

____

____

____

____

____

____

____

____

____

Week 11: Priorities and Balance, Day 1

Walking the thin line

An infinitesimally thin line separates obsession and commitment—between excellence and an insatiable desire to be on top. Cross over the line and you'll pay a steep price.

We addressed commitment the first week of the season. We've examined the biblical precedent that commitments should be chosen carefully and honored fully. But is it possible to become so enslaved to the idea of being number one that we lose perspective, misorder priorities, and in the end, find the victory stand nothing more than a fleeting pleasure?

Chloe didn't start long distance running until her late thirties. Always an athlete, she adapted quickly and trained at the side of an elite ultrarunner. Whatever he did in training, Chloe followed suit. But she had a problem: her body couldn't hold up to the rigors of high mileage. Stress fractures became commonplace. But instead of biding her time, she overcompensated by spending hours on elliptical trainers, stair-steppers, or deep-water running in the pool to preserve fitness. She then fought her way back to top race performances, only to be sidelined by another injury. The cycle repeated itself for over five years.

It was frustrating in many ways, but not just for Chloe. She had a husband and two children. Her job in the medical field was highly stressful and demanding. The family was active in church, teaching Sunday school and singing in the choir. Chloe began burning the candle at both ends and got scorched in the process. She rose at 5:00 a.m. to get in a first run, worked for hours in surgery, ran again, got home late, stayed up to the wee hours to accomplish household tasks, and fell into bed.

She lived, ate, and slept figuring out how to get to the next level of competition. Everything suffered. Her marriage wasn't destroyed, but it was strained. Her role as a mom was compromised due to her exhaustion. Interest in spiritual matters waned. Chloe allowed running excellence and championships to become the driving force in her life. A very bad decision.

A major incident set Chloe's priorities straight. In the ensuing years, she focused on a balanced approach. She didn't train as many hours, and she became more intentional in her role as a wife and a mother. Those changes came from a renewed focus on her spiritual life. She submitted all things—including her running—to God. She learned that running itself was no good unless it brought glory to God, not self.

Team Truth: *It is the Lord Christ you are serving.* (Colossians 3:24b)

Team Time: How can you tell if you've become too obsessed with your sport? Does it necessarily mean you've crossed the line if you sacrifice some things due to training?

Week 11: Priorities and Balance, Day 2

Choose wisely

Life is complicated. Whether we're in school or out, our responsibilities, jobs, teams, hobbies, and "have-tos" battle for our time and attention. In fact, the war can become downright bloody. We stagger off the battlefield, bleeding from the blades of Too-much-to-do and Too-little-time-to-do-it.

How can we fit everything in and get it done without becoming a fallen soldier? Or should the question be this: How can we make wise choices so that the bleeding never starts, so that we're the victors rather than the victims?

Deuteronomy 30 sheds some light on the topic. No, it doesn't talk about whether three hours of practice per day is too much or whether you should also sing in the choir and work in the soup kitchen every Monday night (all of which may be perfectly good things to do). Rather, the chapter conveys a conversation between God and the nation of Israel. It tells us about God's expectations and the choices that the Israelites made.

The first ten verses describe God's faithfulness in restoring the nation to safety and prosperity. "Even if you have been banished to the most distant land . . . the LORD your God will gather you and bring you back" (Deuteronomy 30:4). But in return He expects His people to follow Him with all their heart and soul. Then comes the reality check: "Now what I am commanding you today is not too difficult for you or beyond your reach . . . No, the word is very near you; it is in your mouth and in your heart so you may obey it" (vv. 11, 14). In other words, God had equipped His people to execute His plans.

But still, choices had to be made. One or the other, not both: "See, I set before you today life and prosperity, death and destruction. For I command you today to love the LORD your God, to walk in obedience to him, and to keep his commands, decrees and laws; then you will live and increase, and the LORD your God will bless you in the land you are entering to possess. But if your heart turns away and you are not obedient . . ." (vv. 15-17). Then what?

"If" is almost always followed by "then" and this is no exception. The "then" was annihilation if they chose disobedience. God asked the Israelites to make a decision of enormous proportions. Reading the historical account, the best choice seems obvious: blessings. Right? Right. Who would choose destruction?

Now, don't be too harsh in your criticism if you read further in the book and see poorly made decisions. We also fail to see the obvious as we make our own choices. So the point is this: decisions we make and commitments we embrace always have consequences. Does each choice turn our hearts toward God or away from Him? Choose wisely.

Team Truth: *I have set before you life and death, blessings and curses. Now choose life, so that you and your children may live and that you may love the LORD your God, listen to his voice, and hold fast to him.* (Deuteronomy 30:19b-20a)

Team Time: If we don't love, listen, and hold to God, we cannot choose wisely. Can you think of a bad choice you made because you failed to do these things?

Week 11: Priorities and Balance, Day 3

Now stop it!

The quick-paced soccer drill demanded the concentration of each player in order to rehearse the set play with any level of success. Things went well until one of the players, Meghan, lost focus. She made one mistake after another, which, in turn, messed up the whole sequence.

"Come on," she screamed. "Give me something I can work with!" But clearly, the fault was hers.

After watching from the sidelines for a while, the coach decided to step in. He motioned for the three players in Meghan's group to come for a chat. "What's up, Meghan? Your behavior is unacceptable. I want it to stop."

"Coach. Come on. It's not my fault. If they could shovel a decent ball to me, things would be just fine." Meghan's pitch rose along with her anger.

"I'm not buying it. You're responsible. Go take a seat and think about this for a while. And if I hear another word, you're benched for a week." Coach hoped the downtime would put things back into perspective for Meghan. She was a good kid and a good player, but her behavior was out of line.

A similar situation occurred long ago. Moses, Aaron, and Miriam—the three siblings God chose to lead Israel out of captivity—had their own set of problems. At one point, Aaron and Miriam were miffed that Moses seemed to be God's top dog. In fact, they started to pick him apart, trash-talking him and his Cushite wife. God came down in a cloud pillar and essentially said, "I hear you. Shame on you!" By the time He finished speaking, Miriam had a bad case of leprosy.

"Please, God. Don't hold our sin against her," Aaron pleaded.

"Yes. Please, God. Heal her!" Moses begged on behalf of his sister.

God's response? "Nope. She has to learn her lesson. Send her out of the camp for seven days. After that, she'll be healed of her disease and she can come back."

So, that's the way it was. Miriam left camp for a week, forcing the entire nation to halt their travels. Everyone had time to think about actions and consequences. When she returned, relationships, as well as her skin, were healed.

God forgave them instantly when they asked, but there was still a price to pay. God never stopped loving them. They just needed a timeout to refocus.

Sometimes, we need a timeout as well.

Team Truth: *"Confine her outside the camp for seven days; after that she can be brought back." So Miriam was confined outside the camp for seven days, and the people did not move on till she was brought back.* (Numbers 12:14b-15)

Team Time: Being disciplined is tough. It hurts. And it can be embarrassing. But sometimes it's necessary. Describe a time of discipline that made you a better person.

____

____

____

____

____

____

____

____

____

Week 11: Priorities and Balance, Day 4

Self what?

Off the field, people called him the Gentle Giant. On the field? Not so much.

Derrick was the head coach of a top-ranked high school football program. He spent four years as a star on his college team before fulfilling his dream of playing in the NFL. He certainly knew football and after his pro career ended, he enjoyed teaching the game to his young protégés. He spent countless hours reviewing game video and planning practices. When Derrick left his office to roam the hallways, his smiles and pleasant greetings gave rise to the nickname for this physically dominating man.

But come Friday night, a different man emerged. He screamed, ranted, and raved from the sidelines. His athletes cowered in his presence when he got in their face. On occasion, the local TV cameras caught a few choice words spewing from his mouth. He slammed clipboards into the lockers during halftime and dented more than a few doors with his foot.

One night, the athletic director approached him. "Derrick.

What's with the rage? You're sending the wrong message to your players and to the fans. Get a grip."

"George. Come on now. This is who I am. It's my personality. I just happen to be an intense kind of guy. Everyone knows that and besides, it's all part of the game." With that, Derrick turned away and refocused on the field. "Get with it, Jason!" he shouted to his defensive tackle. "Get your big piece of lard moving!"

So what do you think? Is a split personality appropriate for a coach (or a player)? Is that behavior acceptable in a game setting? Just chalk it up to personality? Not if we understand the importance of self-control.

Paul wrote to Titus long ago. The letter contains an entire discourse on the attributes important for different categories of people. Read the following and determine the common denominator:

- "Teach the older men to be temperate, worthy of respect, *self-controlled,* and sound in faith, in love and in endurance." (Titus 2:1)

- "Likewise, teach the older women to be reverent in the way they live . . . Then they can urge the younger women to love their husbands and children, to *be self-controlled* and pure . . ." (Titus 2:3-5)

- "Similarly, encourage the young men to be *self-controlled.*" (Titus 2:6)

God expects everyone, old and young alike, to practice

self-control—at all times. So why do so many of us rationalize our behavior when we step onto the field or court?

Team Truth: *Like a city whose walls are broken through is a person who lacks self-control.* (Proverbs 25:28)

Team Time: Doing our best for God's glory requires focus and intensity. What's the difference between focused intensity and losing self-control? Give an example.

Week 11: Priorities and Balance, Day 5

Remember when

Always looking forward can make us lose perspective. "Remember when" can put priorities back in order.

In 445 BC, Nehemiah was the cupbearer to Artaxerxes, king of Persia. Through a series of events, Nehemiah, a Jew, adopted the life goal of rebuilding Jerusalem. Making the city a stronghold again required a lot of sweat. But finally, the work was completed and the people gathered for a daylong event.

The people—all of them—came together wearing rags and covering their heads in ashes, a sign of humility. Nehemiah 9 records that they stood for a quarter of the day listening as the Book of the Law was read aloud. For the next quarter (think six hours!) they responded to the command, "Stand up and praise the LORD your God, who is from everlasting to everlasting" (v. 5). They recounted all that happened in their storied history.

It went something like this: "You alone are God . . . you give life . . . you have kept your promise . . . you are faithful . . . you saw our suffering . . . you sent signs to Pharaoh . . .

you gave our people laws . . . you led us . . . you fed us."

But, and there is always a "but," the people also recalled their ancestors' screw-ups. They had become arrogant, stubborn, disobedient, and rebellious. Occasionally, they repented and gave themselves back to God—but not for long. The cycle was repeated over and over. The writer says, however, "But in your great mercy you did not put an end to them or abandon them, for you are a gracious and merciful God . . . In all that has happened to us, you have remained righteous; you have acted faithfully, while we acted wickedly" (vv. 31-33).

Can you imagine hundreds of thousands of people gathered together listening to the Law, praising God, and remembering stories of the past? It must have been a very powerful event. But the question is why? Why did they spend all that time and effort remembering the past? Looking at where they came from put where they were going in perspective.

In life, including sports, an occasional glance over our shoulder is beneficial. We can see progress that's been made. It's like climbing to the top of a mountain and being absolutely amazed when you turn and see where you started, far away and down in the valley.

But getting back to our story. Do you know what the people did after all of that remembering? They took action. They made a commitment, in writing, that they would follow God in the days to come. Considering the past set the course for their future.

Team Truth: *In view of all this, we are making a binding agreement,[and] putting it in writing.* (Nehemiah 9:38a)

Team Time: What kind of history does your team have? What past events have impacted your team, positively or negatively? Does the team need to write or reconfirm their resolutions?

____

____

____

____

____

____

____

____

____

____

Week 12: Finishing Fitness, Day 1

Recommit and lead

Coach looked at the calendar and groaned. Two more weeks. Ugh! It seemed like the longest season ever. A mountain of pressing things needed attention at home, and work-related responsibilities were at an all-time high. Coming up with anything but the same old drills for practice was more and more difficult. The players were listless and tired, dragging into practice with about the same enthusiasm as a prisoner walking to the gallows. To end the season on a high note, something had to change.

But what? What could help the coach and her team become rejuvenated and finish out the season with heads held high? The only hope was a renewed commitment—and that had to come from the top.

Coach picked up her Bible, absentmindedly flipping through the Old Testament. Something caught her eye in 2 Kings 23. The king of Judah, Amon, was brutally murdered in 641 BC. According to law, his son inherited the throne. The son, Josiah, however, was a scrawny eight-year-old kid. Still, a rule was a rule. He was appointed king and he reigned for the next thirty-one years.

Josiah was a good king despite the fact that his grandfather was known for turning the nation away from God and opening the temple to idol worship. Josiah knew that was wrong and set about fixing it. He got rid of the idols and lewd practices that had become common in the temple. In the process, an ancient, dusty scroll, "The Book of the Law," was found. Josiah ordered it read out loud to all the people. Few had any knowledge of it because it had been hidden away for many years. So powerful was its message that Josiah renewed his own commitment to follow the true God with all of his heart and soul. Apparently, the effect on Josiah was profound: the people's hearts were also changed. They, too, decided to obey and worship God alone.

The point is this: sometimes all it takes is for one person to step up. Josiah's decision to concentrate on the important stuff—obedience to God's law—was the catalyst that turned an entire nation back to its roots. Maybe it's time for someone—perhaps the coach, or a senior, or the captain—to refocus on what's really important. Someone needs to fully use their talents to point others to God, to reflect His glory, and to bring honor to Him.

Who will be the first to renew the commitment? It's likely to be contagious.

Team Truth: *The king stood by the pillar and renewed the covenant in the presence of the LORD—to follow the LORD and keep his commands, statutes and decrees with all his heart and all his soul, thus confirming the words of the covenant written in this book. Then all the people pledged themselves to the covenant.* (2 Kings 23:3)

Team Time: Does your team need renewal? What commitments did you make back in Week One? How are you doing?

____

____

____

____

____

____

____

____

____

Week 12: Finishing Fitness, Day 2

Play hard

By watching the sideline spectators, you could tell what was happening on the field. Some fans paced, a few sat on the edges of their chairs, and others chose vocal support. But all hearts raced as they watched the scene unfold on the pitch.

The New Covenant Schools' soccer team was the proverbial "dream team," so strong was their play in the fall of 2006. That band of brothers (and a few sisters) touted as much passion as technical play. During November, the team had gone undefeated in tournament play at the National Association of Christian Athletes (NACA) in Dayton, TN. Now they faced their nemesis in the championship game.

They had played—and beaten—Fresta Valley before and both teams knew the other well. Fresta double-teamed the two most dangerous players for NCS. Caleb Trittipoe had scored over fifty goals during the season, but he couldn't free himself from his assigned shadows, even with his blazing speed. The mid-field player, Timothy Bullock, also drew constant defenders. He, too, was rendered ineffective.

But the good news was that Seth Trittipoe—the freshman brother of Caleb and a bold, powerhouse player—was not contained. Two times he scored in regulation play. However, as the clock ticked down, Fresta found the back of the net—twice. The game was tied at two. Double five-minute overtimes would decide who carried the trophy from the field.

The play was frantic, each team straining with all their might to score. Everyone assumed Caleb or Timothy would eventually break loose to bag the winning goal. After all, they were the go-to players, finessed and skilled. In contrast, Seth's success—the season's second highest scorer—came as a result of intensity, speed, and raw fearlessness. But could a freshman really be the hero and score the winner?

Three minutes into the first overtime period it happened. Seth made a crazy run and drilled the ball. Spectators rose in unison as the ball arched toward the goal. Time stood still until the ball ricocheted against the back of the net. NCS led 3-2. They had to hold on for another seven minutes.

When the final buzzer sounded, Seth had done the unthinkable. A ninth grader claimed all three scores in a championship game. It wasn't his skill—others had more—or calculated play. No. It was his decision to play all-out, drawing on every ounce of athleticism he had. He never assumed someone else would get the job done. He never quit. He held onto hope. He gave all he had to offer. He knew how to end a season.

Team Truth: *But one thing I do: Forgetting what is behind and straining toward what is ahead, I press on toward the goal to win the prize for which God has called me heavenward in Christ Jesus.* (Philippians 3:13b-14)

Team Time: Certainly, every Christian should strive to earn God's prize. But in principle, does the way you play a game have anything to do with this verse?

____

____

____

____

____

____

____

____

____

____

Week 12: Finishing Fitness, Day 3

Don't give up now

She looked at her watch. Her mind whirled trying to manipulate the numbers. *Hmm. The race ends at 6:00 p.m. and I have over six miles to go. Let's see, what time is it now? Wow! With three of those miles straight up, I don't know if I can make it in time. It's gonna be tough.* The pit in her stomach grew as she thought about missing the cutoff.

Stacy had been running for over sixteen hours and was totally whipped. Her stomach revolted and her legs felt stiff—unlikely candidates to carry her up, over, and down the mountain. She had a love-hate relationship with this race, the Hellgate 100K. It starts at one minute after midnight on the second Saturday in December. The weather always proves unpredictable and the terrain through the Blue Ridge Mountains is unforgiving. But Stacy had started every race, had more finishes than any other woman, and wanted to keep it that way. She had to keep moving.

She started up the last climb of the brutal race. Precious seconds kept ticking away. She was exhausted physically and mentally, having run all through the night and day. Pulling the plug on this race down at the bottom of the mountain would've felt good. But Stacy had suffered too long and hard to quit so close to the end. If she had, all that pain would've been for naught.

When she crested the mountain and crossed the road for the final descent, she glanced at her watch. She was surprised to see she had substantial time remaining. "I must have miscalculated," she mused. The pressure was off; she knew that even a slow run from there would earn a finisher's award. But still, she felt conflicted. She could back off and slide in under the wire for the finish. She wasn't in the hunt to place well or set a personal record. Not even close. Or she could do her best with whatever she had left. The latter was the harder choice. It meant choosing to hurt more. But still, it seemed like her efforts of the last sixteen-plus hours would be wasted if she yielded to the pain.

Stacy dug deep and finished the race using up her last bit of strength. It was a personal worst finish, but a personal success at the same time. Stacy held it together in the last remaining moments, taking advantage of what she found deep inside.

Jesus actually taught the same principle. In a discourse with a crowd, He hinted at His impending crucifixion. He said, "Take advantage of me while I'm still here. I am the light. Walk with me in the light before I leave and the darkness comes. Hold on while you can" (paraphrased).

It's easy to quit near the end—but don't! Take advantage

of what you have left and finish strong while you have the chance.

Team Truth: *Then Jesus told them, "You are going to have the light just a little while longer. Walk while you have the light, before darkness overtakes you . . . Believe in the light while you have the light, so that you may become children of light."* (John 12:35-36)

Team Time: Let's assume your team had a losing season. No championships are on the line. How can you still finish strong?

____

____

____

____

____

____

____

____

____

____

Week 12: Finishing Fitness, Day 4

Carry on

The athletes gathered in their usual meeting place, a tiny hallway in the back recesses of the school. The cross country team didn't get a lot of respect or recognition. In fact, they didn't even have a home course or track to call their own. Few spectators, save a handful of parents, came to see the runners attack the hills and fly across grassy fields. Still, the team was larger than ever—news of the unique practices and "adventures" had spread enthusiasm for the sport like wildfire.

It was the last practice of the season. Tomorrow the team would compete in the state meet and after that, the uniforms would be collected, accounted for, and put away for another year. The athletes looked forward to the meet and all that went along with it: leaving school early, going for breakfast, a noisy bus ride, the race, and more eating on the way home. And though everyone was tired from months of running and weekend meets, they knew they'd miss being together as a team. They felt like a family. They were a family.

Not all teams love each other. Some teams are marked by

cynicism, jealousy, apathy, and rebellion. Sometimes the coach hates being the coach, which creates a whole different set of problems. But the way a team interacts reveals a lot about the deep-down health of a team. We're not talking about a win-loss record (although a healthy team often produces good results). We're looking at the integrity of each member and their effectiveness when they function as a unit.

A team is like a body with lots of parts: arms, legs, nose, ears, muscles, tendons, fascia, blood cells, and yes, even fat. Each has its vital role and none can perform whole body functions by themselves. Each part must understand the whole task and contribute its services to get the job done. Then and only then, can the body function at its highest level and realize the goal.

Working together as a team (body) is seldom easy. Sometimes a member gets sick and needs to be nursed back to health. For example, a foot becomes numb because it has fallen asleep from inactivity. Getting that foot back in the game is difficult—fighting through tingling pain and weakness, and needing a good dose of rehab in the process. In fact, a well-working body is a full-time job that requires every member's input.

As the season draws to a close, thank each member of your team for their contribution and bring healing to those who struggle. Carry on the good work that has begun.

Team Truth: *Being confident of this, that he who began a good work in you will carry it on to completion until the day of Christ Jesus . . . And this is my prayer: that your love may abound more and more in knowledge and depth of insight, so that you may be able to discern what is best and may be pure and blameless for the day of Christ, filled with the fruit of righteousness that comes through Jesus Christ—to the glory and praise of God.* (Philippians 1:6, 9-11)

Team Time: Is your team functioning as a healthy unit? What can you do to optimize its health even though it's late in the season?

____

____

____

____

____

____

____

____

Week 12: Finishing Fitness, Day 5

After the finish line

A second grade teacher once made a wise distinction when a student said, "Teacher, teacher. I'm done!"

"Cakes get 'done,'" she said. "People get 'finished.'" In the same spirit, we're nearly finished with another season. Does that mean it's all over, *el fin*, *completo*, *nada mas*?

Consider this: finishing one thing ushers in the beginning of something else. Always. No exceptions. For example, the buzzer sounds and the team walks into the locker room. The buzzer marks the finish of the first half but also the beginning of the halftime break. An exhausted runner stumbles across the line after completing a marathon. He's finished with the race, but his recovery is just beginning.

Think about that a little more. If you saw someone complete a task and were asked to write about it, what would you say? "He finished." Period. Or "He finished, and then he . . ."? You'd probably describe what came after the finish as well as the fact of completion.

As we approach the end of the season, we often focus on

the final buzzer, crossing under the finish banner, the end of daily practices, and no more aching muscles. But if we don't look beyond those things, we'll miss something.

Remember when Jesus was crucified? He was nailed to a cross and dying one of the most horrific deaths known to man. Listen to what He said near the end: "Later, knowing that everything had now been finished, and so that Scripture would be fulfilled, Jesus said, 'I am thirsty.' A jar of wine vinegar was there, so they soaked a sponge in it, put the sponge on a stalk of the hyssop plant, and lifted it to Jesus' lips. When he had received the drink, Jesus said, 'It is finished.' With that, he bowed his head and gave up his spirit" (John 19:28-30).

Does that mean there was nothing beyond His last breath? Thank God, no! He was only finished with the specific task of dying for our benefit. Sure, Christ's ministry on earth was over, and He would spend three days in the ground. But after that, He came out of the tomb and later returned to His Father in heaven. Even now, He still isn't finished. He loves, guides, protects, serves as our intercessor to the Father, and matures us as we grow in our faith.

We all get tired and look forward to a "finish." However, we should understand that the finish of one task simply leads to the beginning of another. Without a doubt, we'll enjoy a period of rest. But then, another assignment waits.

Be sure to appreciate the finish but don't lose sight of the next starting gun.

Team Truth: *"My food," said Jesus, "is to do the will of him who sent me and to finish his work."* (John 4:34)

Team Time: What have you learned or developed this season that should continue after the final event? Complete the following: "I'll/we'll finish. Then I'll'/we'll . . ."

____

____

____

____

____

____

____

____

____

____

Acknowledgements

Few things in life are solo efforts, and that includes writing. I was blessed to have several friends join the team to help me deliver a useful and practical book to coaches and athletes alike.

Natalie Olenik, how can I ever thank you? You're a busy wife, mom-in-waiting, teacher, and coach. And yet you took the time to pour over every page of this manuscript to correct and improve the final product. Your insights and suggestions for improvement were invaluable. Thank you so much for your tireless and selfless help. I couldn't have done this without you.

And Lori Flowers, thank you for putting your set of eyes and coach's heart to this project. I appreciate the time you put in to review the work and to provide substantial feedback.

Bob Hostettler and Virelle Kidder. Thank you for the professional encouragement and expertise that you lent to this project. Your kind words and support for this book stay safely tucked into the recesses of my heart.

Bob Hostettler and Virelle Kidder, thank you meeting with me at the Montrose Writers Conference. Your openness to this project was a direct answer to prayer. I appreciate the team you assembled to handle this manuscript, including

Denise Loock's editing genius.

And of course, thanks to Gary Trittipoe, my husband of many years, for your continued support and unquestioned loyalty to my writing, one of my many "projects." I can always count on you!

www.ingramcontent.com/pod-product-compliance
Lightning Source LLC
LaVergne TN
LVHW010615100826
845148LV00014B/2975

9781737089940